Orphaned

then embraced by the caring hands of an
Amish Mennonite family

THE AUTOBIOGRAPHY OF GEORGE MOHLER

ISBN: 0-9776-2130-8
ISBN-13:   9780977621309

Contents

Contents

Acknowledgments

I was told several years ago that since my memory is good I should write my life story. While in Belarus, during the fall of 2002 building a church, I realized it was time. The idea of this book is to tell my daughter and granddaughters of the life I have lived here on earth. I am 69 years old and I have a lot of memories of my childhood days. I have lived at many different places, including an orphanage in Millersville for one year. There are memories that I want to put down on paper before I forget. So herein is a true story of my life. We must all seek God's forgiveness for many things in life. The God of heaven knows my heart's secrets, and some things are closed books. I will, however, share some of my memories, as I feel led.

I want to thank my dear wife and daughter for helping with this book. I dedicate this to my daughter, Nancy, her husband, Jim, and my granddaughters, Lenette and Diana.

George Mohler, 2004

Geography

Located in central Pennsylvania, Belleville is a small town in the center of Big Valley, in Mifflin County. My home was three miles southwest of town, just off Route 655, near a village called White Hall. It is officially called Menno on the road map. My foster mother named our farm, The White Hall Farm. Big Valley is a special place, also known as the Kishacoquillas Valley, and was named after a local Indian chief. It is unique, because it is shaped like a boat—34 miles long and four miles wide at its widest place. We have many Mennonite and Amish folks living here. The valley has Stone Mountain on the north side and Jack's Mountain on the south side. Paul Harvey, a news commentator, once said he had been everywhere, but this is one of the most picturesque places on earth! So, come to Belleville, Pennsylvania, and see our beautiful Big Valley. You may especially enjoy a Wednesday visit at our famous market and auction! Our area was also featured in the *National Geographic* magazine several years ago.

CHAPTER 1

My Earliest Memories

As you look back on your life, it is amazing what you remember. My earliest memories are of my mother, Esther, and a house along a trolley track. I do not remember my father at all, but I know we lived with an uncle in a white house. It was while we lived there that my brother was born. Later we lived somewhere else and my baby sister was born. Later, we came back to my uncle's house to live again.

I have some early memories of living in that house. One time my uncle found a big turtle that he killed and made turtle soup. Another time I took my neighbor's kite and hid it. I wanted it for myself!

Once I laid my brother's rag doll on the trolley

track. When the conductor saw me put the doll on the track, he shook his finger at me. I was so scared that I never did it again. Another time, I remember coming down the steps. Mother was washing the floor and I accidentally put my foot in the bucket of hot water, scalding my foot. I must have been four years old at the time.

Another memory is meeting a big man who was walking down the street. I said to him, "You are so black, why don't you take a bath!" He said that if I said that again, he would cut my ears off. I remember running into the house, crying for my mother. She explained that God made people in different colors.

When I was six, I remember riding in the rumble seat of my uncle's car. Mother was in the front holding my baby sister, and my brother sat beside me. We

My mother, Esther, and George.

went on a ride to a new place. It was an orphanage in Millersville, Pennsylvania, owned and operated by the Mennonite Church.

Little Nancy, Bobby, and George Kloepfer.

CHAPTER 2

My Home Away From Home

As best, as I can recall, my brother, sister, and I arrived at this new "home" in the late summer of 1939. I remember two older men well. Simon Heistand was the superintendent of the home and Gideon Eberly was in charge of the boys. I remember some of the good times and painful times.

There was a long wooden table where we would sit and eat our meals. We used metal pie plates. There was a brick orphanage schoolhouse close behind the main building where the older children attended classes and in the fall of 1941, I began first grade. Right beside the school was a sand box where we could play. Every Sunday we were dressed in our best, and we would walk down the long lane to the big church called Millersville Mennonite Church

We were given little projects to do so we would learn the meaning of responsibility. One thing that we boys would do was take cans with some liquid in it and go catch and kill Japanese beetles that we collected off of the hedge which paralleled the lane to the home. We thought that was a lot of fun and not really a job.

There was a large white painted barn close to the home. I would go there and help feed the pigs and gather eggs. Sometimes the chickens would pick the top of my hand and it hurt.

It has been said that children may wet their beds when they are under stress. One day Mr. Eberly was very cross with me because I wet my bed. He took his belt off and whipped me. It was very painful! I guess he thought that experience would help my bladder control problem.

I can remember my uncle and mother bringing us toys and candy, especially at Christmas time. Once they gave me a little train and another time a sailor suit. I have memories of my brother and sister in the home, but we were soon separated and placed in different foster homes. Gradually my mother's visits became less and less.

CHAPTER 3

We Are Separated

In the spring of 1942, a lady by the name of Katie Mae Kauffman, from Belleville, Pennsylvania, stopped at the orphanage. I was seven years old at that time and I well remember that I had just been to the hospital to have my tonsils removed. I still can see the black thing that they put over my nose and mouth that made me breathe some bad smelling stuff. Later, when I could think again, the nurse asked me if I wanted something to eat and I said I wanted some ice cream. She said, "Oh no, that would not be good for you. I will give you some prune juice!"

When Mrs. Kauffman came, the superintendent said, "Why don't you take this little boy along home with you? He just had his tonsils out and it would be good for him to get out to a new place and fresh air."

So they dressed me in my sailor suit that my real mother had gotten for me, and along with all my belongings, I went with this new woman to Belleville. I told her, "I don't want to go back to that place again!"

Katie Mae, as my new mother would now be called, was forty-one years old when she took me to raise. Later she told me that she was born in 1900, and had married a young man in 1921. His name was David Yoder. However, he soon died pitching sheaves of grain on the wagon during the summer harvest, and she became a widow. A few years later, she met a man from the Lancaster area, whose name was Daniel B. Kauffman. His wife had died earlier, leaving him with three children. Therefore, mother married him. I have only met his children a few times, as they were much older than I was. It was shortly before Katie Mae took me to raise that Mr. Kauffman died, so now she was a widow for the second time.

My new mother had taken a number of people into her home to live for different periods of time. It was a big, fifteen-room farmhouse that was heated with six fireplaces in the 1800s but now had a boiler to heat the house. She told me that some rich people, John Clark and Hannah Mary Wilson, built the house in 1836. There is still a plaque built into the outside wall with their names painted on it.

I was excited to be in this big place. There was so much for a seven-year-old boy to explore. In addition, since she owned a big farm, she needed lots of help with the chores. Mother soon had things for me to do.

*An arial view of the farm at White Hall that was my home
for 15 years as a boy.*

Mother told me about her two sisters, Sadie and Ada, and her brother, Steve. Her father had purchased this big farm in 1890. Mother's two sisters lived on farms right next to her farm, so she could shout very loudly to her sisters. Mother could whistle very loudly too. She would put her two little fingers at the edge of her mouth and the sound could be heard a half mile away.

Mother was a good shot with her little rifle. She had inherited a 32-20-caliber rifle from her father. Mother would shoot the groundhogs that got into the truck patch. She would clean them and we would eat them. Mother showed me a little yellow colored gland under their front leg that she would remove as soon as she skinned them. Later when mother died and her possessions were sold, I bought the 32-

20. It was a Winchester model 1892 lever action. I hunted deer with it for many years. Recently I sold it, but down deep in my heart, I wish I had it back for my memories' sake.

One day, Mother came home with a tub of eels. They looked a little like snakes, but she cleaned them and we ate them. They were not too bad, but there are much better things to eat than eels!

We had a telephone on the wall that you picked up this black part and put it against your ear. Then you turned a crank on the wall, and soon a person in Belleville said, "What number do you want?" Mother would often say "R4" and then she would wait a moment while the operator would pull a wire from one place and stick it into another spot. Soon she would be talking to Roy Stuck, who owned a feed mill in Belleville! It was customary for five or six families to share what was called a party line; you learned to take turns using the phone. One day Mother took me to Belleville to see the woman who worked in the telephone exchange building where she moved the wires around. I think the woman's name was Goldie Kauffman. This is the way the telephone systems operated in the middle forties.

Many of the farmhouses had a built-on addition, called the grandfather house. As the children grew older and got married, the parents would move into the new addition and then be cared for by the younger generation. Since Mother's parents were deceased, she had a young family living in this addition to help with the chores. Their names were Abe and Hannah Yoder and they had several boys. Abe's little boys would climb up on the fence, call over to Mother's cook, and ask for candy. Annie, as she was called, would take some out for them.

Mother soon had us children going barefoot in the spring. This saved wear and tear on the shoes, and it seemed to make our feet healthier. I soon had hard calluses on the bottom of my feet. I just hated to run over a field of dried hay, because those dried cut alfalfa stubs would punch your feet and that would hurt. When you walked over a new field of clover, you would not see the honeybees until they stung you under the toes.

We would go barefoot until late in the fall. I remember when the grass was white with frost, I would go out for the cows early in the morning, I would go step in the fresh cow piles just to get my feet warm. One morning I was so sleepy I lay down in the spot where a cow had just gotten up and soon went to sleep in that warm spot. I was rudely awakened later and growled for not bringing the cows in to the barn like I was supposed to.

In the summer time, I would go in the grain fields and pull the bad weeds out. Wild carrots, yellow mustard, and chicory weeds were the hardest things to kill. I mowed many patches of thistles, too. Mother did not want those weeds to go to seed and she complained about the neighbors that did let their weed seeds go wild.

CHAPTER 4

A New Life on the Farm

My new mother was a devout Mennonite lady, and time was set aside every morning, seven days a week, right after breakfast to read the Bible, each taking a turn reading a verse. Then we would sing a song or two from the book called "Life Songs" that had over 300 songs. I learned most of them. Afterwards, we got down on our knees and we learned to pray! (NOTE: This is something that millions of children should be taught. It would be a much better world.) It did not matter if there were salesmen waiting in the driveway or if the telephone would ring, they had to wait until we were done praying.

There was a single man named Samuel Y. Peachey

that lived at the farm when I came there. Mother's father had taken him as a young boy, because his parents had some stressful times in their life. They had four children, three boys and one girl, who died from gangrene in an accident with a corn chopper. Therefore, Sammie, as everyone called him, became my best friend. He was 26 years older than I was, but that did not matter. He taught me about the farm animals and helped me to understand the Bible. We took walks in the mountains and I learned some of the history of the Valley, but one thing he never talked about was girls. It seemed to me that subject was never talked about, although my mother did give me a book titled "What a Young Boy Ought to Know". It apparently did not mean much to me because I do not remember much about it.

Mother's father, Mose, had taken in another poor

Katie Mae and Lizzie working in the winter kitchen.

Amish girl to help with the farm and housework. Her name was Elizabeth Ann Hostetler. She was born in 1912 to David and Barbara Hostetler, their only child. Lizzie, as everyone called her, was not as bright as some; in fact, she could not complete her elementary education. Reading was a real problem, but Mother was patient with her. She could cook, work the garden, bake bread, and help with the other chores.

Mother also took another girl from the orphanage named Martha Price just before she took me. Mother named her Anna Martha, and since she was just a year or so younger than I was, we became like brother and sister.

The first picture taken of George and Martha on the rail fence behind the barn at the farm.

George and Martha beside the flowers.

Martha, George, and Jane who is 11 years younger.

In 1948, Mother took another girl to raise from the Lewistown area. Her name was Janie and she was only two years old at the time. Mother officially adopted her. She was the only child of all the children that Mother raised that she legally adopted. There had also been several of Mother's nephews that also came to work on the farm before I came there.

Mother taught us children the Pennsylvania Dutch language. Since we were small, it was easy for us to learn. There were a lot of Amish people living all around us and in school so it was so nice to speak their language too. (In later years, my wife and I spoke more Dutch at home than we did English!)

Mother raised German Shepherds to sell. We had two dogs that she kept for watchdogs: a female named Duchess, and a male named Traveler, who lived

My pets, Traveler on my left and Duchess on my right.

many years. I will never forget one particular day, as we came in from the field to eat lunch, Traveler went to his doghouse. When we came back out of the house to do the chores, Traveler got out of his house, gave a big yawn, and fell over dead! Sammie and I cried over that. We had to bury him, so we dug a nice grave under the big tree behind the barn for Traveler.

Sammie and my favorite German Shepherd, Traveler, taken in 1950.

In 1942, I began my education at the White Hall School. This was a one-room building with a big stove in the corner that heated the room. As the smaller children and I came in the front door, the older children told us that if we would not behave they would put us down the alligator hole. We found out later that the hole was an access hole to go under the floor. The teacher had to be a person with a lot of variety. She would start in the morning with prayer and sometimes a song. Then she would begin with the first grade class and gradually move up to the eighth grade. There were a number of Amish children in the class. At that time, the Amish church did not have as many of their own private schools. I remember there were two pictures above the black board. One was an oval shaped picture of George Washington; the other was a picture of a man sitting at a table with his head bowed saying grace before his meal.

For a number of years we received a paper in school called *My Weekly Reader.* This was very interesting to us because it told about things going on in the world that otherwise were not mentioned in our classes. During the war years, a man from the government visited our school and he said that our school could make some money collecting milkweed pods when they were ready to harvest. This man told us that the fluffy stuff in the pods would be used for insulating clothing for the soldiers. We really tried to go around all the fields and fencerows and fill the cloth bags that the man had given us. We felt that we were really helping our country!

There was a big hill going up to the school from the farm. In the wintertime, the snow would be packed down from the traffic. Mother gave me a brand new sled called "The Lightning Glider." It was built very strong and seemed to go very fast. Since some children did not have a sled, they would crawl on top of me. You would not believe the speed that we got going down that long hill with three children on top of that sled, one on top of the other. My sled had a strong wooden bar around it so they could hold on.

The White Hall School where I attended from 1942 until 1948.

We boys liked to dig caves in the deep snowdrifts. We wanted to show the girls our nice caves but the teacher said that we were not allowed to have the girls in our caves! I guess she knew more about life than we did! I loved to read books, especially mystery books like Nancy Drew and Hardy Boys, and stories about cowboys and Indians. At lunchtime, I would run down the big hill to our house and eat lunch at home. Mother always had a few chores for me to do right after I finished eating so I had to rush around doing them, which would make me late for the one o'clock period. Then as punishment, I could not play ball and other things at recess! This would frustrate me.

I tried to be a good student, but I remember that I got a spanking once from the teacher. And to make matters worse, when we got home, my younger sister told Mother that I got a spanking in school. This was not very nice of her to say anything about it because I then got a spanking from Mother after supper. What a way to learn!

The long days of hard work and going to school caused me to go to sleep sometimes between classes. The teacher told Mother that I seemed to be so tired all the time. Mother decided that maybe there was something wrong with my mental abilities. Plans were made to take me to a psychiatrist in State College for some tests. I think I was twelve at the time.

This woman would sit down with me and show me some pictures and would ask me what did I see in those pictures. Also, I drew pictures of animals and other things. Finally, the psychiatrist told Mother that I needed more rest. She said that I seemed to be a very healthy boy, but was suffering from lack of sleep. She asked Mother when I got up in the morning, when I went to bed, and what all my daily tasks were. The psychiatrist told Mother that was too much for a boy to do at this age. Now this did not go over to well with Mother. She decided to take me out of school for one week and see what would happen. I still had to get up early in the morning, chase the cows in from the fields, help with the chores, come in and eat breakfast, then go to bed. Mother would wake me up at noon for dinner. I would go and do a few chores, and go back to bed until suppertime. When supper was over, I would help with the work and go to bed early. I did this for one week. After that, it was back to the old schedule again. I knew that Mother was not too happy knowing that people would find out that she worked us all to hard, but that was part of my young life. Even the neighbors complained to each other how George and Martha seemed to be slaves to her.

Our teachers' names from 1941-1950 were Bertha Leasea, Lucille Leasea, Mary Laub, Emma Patton, and Janet Huey, who are all deceased now. I spent all but two years of my education at the White Hall School. Then the school closed for good and was purchased by Jesse Peachey and remodeled for a home. I then went to Allensville Elementary School to finish seventh and eighth grades. I want to say here that Mother was not satisfied with my knowledge of the multiplication tables so she made me take seventh grade over again! I was bored with school, although I excelled in history, geography, and spelling. English was my worst. I had trouble with nouns, pronouns, adjectives, and adverbs. To this day, I still do not know them and do not really care, but it would have come in handy when writing this book! I remember the last day of school very well when our teacher, Janet Huey, said, "School is over. Be sure to pick up your report cards." I went out the door and ran the whole way home, which was four miles. I had changed clothes and was going to the barn as the bus was going down the road!

This was the end of my schooling. Mother said that high school was for city kids and I was needed on the farm so I never went any farther in my studies. (Years later, after I was married, I took a course in highway construction and design and did well until

I got to the section about the power of square roots and approximate numbers, and then I quit.)

Each month on the last Thursday I had to take a laxative. I did not like this stuff, called "Swiss Kriss." It was made from many kinds of herbs. Now that in itself is alright, but one teaspoon of that would give you an extreme bellyache. I wish to say that when I was married and moved away from home, the laxative stayed behind! One thing for sure, it did clean you out.

One day I got a sore tooth. Mother said that she would pull it out with a strong string, which she then fastened to the door latch and the other end around my tooth. Mother said she would count to three, slowly, so I tried to prepare myself, but mother jerked it at number two and the tooth was out!

CHAPTER 5

Adjusting to Farm Work

Since we lived near the village called White Hall, Mother decided to name our farm The White Hall Farm. She had a friend in Huntingdon who made signs with glass reflective beads that would reflect the light. She put the sign at the end of our long lane. It is sad to say that the sign was not up long before someone in a devilish mood painted the sign red! My mother eventually found out who did it. She prayed for him and forgave him. This taught me about the power of forgiveness. It is so nice to know that God will forgive people if they ask him.

One time when a cow gave birth I looked close to see if it was a bull calf or heifer calf. Now as I looked back at this time, it seemed so silly but as I looked at this calf, I noticed it had four small teats as well as the big testicle of a bull calf. I thought this was a very strange calf and I ran in to the house to mother and told her that the calf was a heifer and bull calf at the same time. Mother looked so astonished and she said, "Really?"

I said, "Come and see!" She did and she chuckled about that. Well, a person has to learn about the genders of animals sometime! I later realized that men have the same location of breasts that women have but ours are not functional like women's are. It did seem unusual, though, for a young boy.

We had two workhorses on the farm named Kate and Pearl. We also had a pony named Nellie. Now I must say Nellie was a very smart pony. I would ride bareback most of the time and I would go out in the pasture field to bring the cows in to milk. Occasionally, Nellie decided she did not want a rider that day and she would winnie and throw me off, especially when she would walk across the creek. So you see, she was temperamental at times.

Mother had a John Deere model B tractor, besides the two workhorses. One time Mother decided to buy another larger tractor, a John Deere model A. Now to me, that was an awesome machine! It could pull three or four plows at a time and we would use this big tractor to run the Dellinger feed grinding machine. Often we would make our own hog, cow, and chicken feed. Mother would buy all the minerals, powdered whey, and meat scraps. I tasted this stuff and some of it was good! No wonder the animals liked it! I did not like to grind old corncobs, because they would make a terrible racket and it was hard on your ears! Occasionally a bolt or piece of steel would get in the grinder and I would rush out to the tractor and disengage the clutch real quick. It made an awful racket.

One day in the late forties or early fifties, Mother decided to buy a brand new Farmall "Cub" tractor to plow the truck patch and pull the wagons. We also used the tractor to pull the hay up from the wagon into the haymow on pulleys. We had used our horse, Pearl, to pull the long hay rope. It was all the big horse could do. I would guide the horse with the bridle. Now when Mother bought this new "Cub International" tractor we said goodbye to the two big workhorses. I just loved to drive that little tractor. It was just like a big toy. Mother purchased a single bottom plow, cultivators, a sickle bar mower, and a power take-off pulley for it so we could saw firewood on a buck saw. One of my jobs was to change the equipment on this machine when she wanted to do something.

In the early forties and before, there was an Amish man that owned a big thrashing machine that he would use to take around to farms in the area to thrash the grain during harvest time. We all tried to schedule the times so this man would arrive at our farm when our grain was ready. I must say, that the neighboring farmers would help each other out. For instance, we would go to Jake Peachey's, then Crist Renno's, then Joe Byler's, then to David Yoder's, and several more to help out, not necessarily in that order. Those days were wonderful times that people of today know nothing about. The fellowship and the food that was served at the different homes was wonderful.

There was a story that used to be told that there

was one farm that the threshers used to go to where the woman was very conservative with her meals. So one day when all the men had finished eating and all the dishes were empty, she said, "I see that I made just the right amount of food. You ate it all!" I guess she must have not been very bright, because the men were all still hungry.

One day Mother got frustrated because the men could not come to our farm when she wanted them to, so she said she was not going to wait. She left in her car, and the next day, a brand new Frick thrashing machine on a big truck came up our lane! So now, we went to the different farms to help them for a while! Mother said this machine cost $4,000 and we must take care of it.

She saw that I was mechanically inclined so she gave me the book about the machine and I was told to study it, so I would know where all the grease fittings were located and to make sure that all the pulleys were running in the right direction. I have many memories of those days hooking up the big tractor with the long drive belt. I was the one to stand on the wagon and throw the sheaves of grain on the feed belt.

One day I decided to try and duplicate this machine, so I spent a lot of time in our little farm shop making pulleys, cutting wood, bending metal and pulling it all together! It was about seven inches wide and 2 feet long. I then carved a tractor out of pinewood to look like a John Deere and put a steering wheel on it to turn the front wheels, plus a gear box and a hand crank to turn the drive pulley real fast. I would hook this to the thrashing machine. I made all the belts out of strips of good strong inner tubes. I would tie eight to ten heads of wheat in little sheaves and lay them on the feeding belt. The cutters would then cut the string and the grains would go into the concaves. The straw would fly out the back blower and the wheat would go up an elevator on the side and down into a bin. (NOTE: In my late forties, after moving several times, I said to my wife, "It is time to get rid of a lot of childhood stuff." So, as we were burning things, I threw the machine in the fire. As soon as it hit the flames, I knew that I had done a terrible thing, which I have regretted to this day. That machine should be on a shelf in my home!)

I used to like to take clocks apart and see if I could put them together again. Sometimes they worked and sometimes they did not!

My mother had a large outdoor bake oven made of bricks with a large cast iron door. Irvin Roth built this. He and his father were well known in the

Katie Mae and Martha standing in front of the bake oven with a fresh loaf of bread.

area as excellent masons and their names are on many sidewalks in our area. In the summer, when garden produce was growing, Mother, Lizzie, and Anna Martha would bake bread, pies, and cakes on Tuesday. It was my job to help Sammie fill this oven with wood scraps on Monday so we would light the fire on Tuesday morning. When the wood was all burned up, we would take a big scraper and take the ashes out, leaving the glowing red-hot bricks. We would then fill this oven with thirty or more loaves of bread, plus pies and cakes.

While they were baking, Sammie and I would clean our pickup truck bed and then lift a glass showcase onto the bed. When the bread was done baking and still very hot, homemade butter was spread all over the top of the bread. This would help prevent it from drying out. Then we would load the showcase with the baked goods and Mother, Anna Martha, and I would go to Huntingdon. Pa. We would pull in at 423 Penn Street beside Black's Jewelry Store, where the people would be waiting to buy the produce and baked goods. This is something we did every week all summer long until the produce was all.

We also sold cherries that we picked from the trees planted along the fencerow behind the house. Sammie and I would pick lots of cherries to take along to market. Sometimes if we still had produce towards the afternoon, Mother would drive up to 8th and 9th Streets, where we children would go door-to-door and soon sell everything. Mother always had real nice cabbage, lettuce, red beets, and onions, so it was no problem to sell them. Anna Martha and I said if we put big smiles on our faces, people would buy them, even if they did not need them.

I did do something one time that I was very sorry for and I will share it. Mother had planted ten small plants of endive in the garden so later we would put it in the cave and we would have endive to eat over winter. Now these plants grew very big, two plants would fill a bushel basket. When Mother would make endive for a meal, she cooked it in a sauce, which had a flavor that I simply did not like! It was terrible and I decided one day I did not want to eat that endive. So, I put just a little weed killer in the center of the plant to see what would happen.

A week or so later, the ten stalks began to turn brown and mother could not understand why the plants appeared to have a blight. Later she was in the shed getting the can of weed killer to kill some weeds. I heard my name being called and I came to the shed. As I entered the shed, she looked at me, holding the can of weed killer up for me to see, and said, "Did you use this on the endive?"

I got this terrible lump in my throat and I said, "Yes." She did not say another word, but began to cry. Oh, how I wished at that moment that the deed could have been undone. As I am writing this, I am having a flash back about it and I am misty eyed because I can still see her face as I walked in that shed door.

The only thing that was good about the whole affair was that we did not have any endive to eat that winter, and I did not get a licking. However, the tears in her eyes were a lot worse than a licking. It goes to say that some things you do are permanent and can not be undone, but I can guarantee that when you ask the Savior Jesus Christ to forgive you for what you do, you do not have that problem to haunt you all your life.

Mother did punish us when we did not obey her. I remember being told that I must go out to the apple tree and cut a switch. The thickness of the stick determined how hard it would hit. If it were thin, it would really sting. So I guess you might say that it hurt either way! This happened a couple of times in my life. One time when mother was mad at Anna Martha, she made her put her hand on the hot stove. That had to hurt badly because she got blisters on her hands.

Once, when we told a fib, Mother made us put hot peppers in our mouths and hold it for a few minutes. We just about gagged! I learned along with the other people that grew up under Mother's rule that you had to do as she said or else.

In the fall of 1954, something happened that I want to share. I shall change the names to protect the innocent. Mother and Dad had a cabin on their mountain ground. She rented it out to hunters during the deer season. One year some hunters from the Lancaster, Pennsylvania, area rented the cabin. This was not appreciated by some of the local farmers who hunted the same area, it seemed that out-of-towners were not welcomed in these parts! One evening one of the farmers took some dynamite sticks and slid them under the foundation of the cabin by the door. The next morning the hunters discovered it there. They wasted no time coming to mother's house and showed her what they found. Mother soon found out who did it.

That evening Mother made the man come to our house. Before he came, she had the hunters come there first. This was a very scary thing for me, because I did not know what could happen. The man, who put the dynamite there, came and cried for mercy from Mother and Dad. He also asked forgiveness from the hunters and they forgave him. I am sure it was a learning experience for him, as well as a scary thing for me.

One of the important things to do each year was to whitewash the board fences around the barnyard and a few other places. We also did some of the fruit tree trunks, mother said the whitewash would delay the sap from going up the trunks so early in the spring. If we would have a late frost, then it would not freeze the buds so quick. Mother would buy a 100-pound bag of slacking lime and I would pour it into a big wooden barrel half full of water. Then it would get very hot. Later when it cooled off, I would take a bucket of this and a whitewash brush and cover everything that mother wanted, even some stone walls. The farm looked so nice after I did this.

One of my daily chores was cleaning the cow stables. We had a track fastened on to the ceiling between the stalls, where a carrier bucket was hung. I would shovel the ditches out and fill the carrier, then I would push it out of the barn and dump it on to the spreader. In the winter, we had a big pit that we would use for this when it was too cold for spreading in the fields.

We had a carrier that could use the same track to take three ten-gallon milk cans to the milk house. There I would drop the cans into a big tank of cold water to cool them down. We would have ten to twelve cans of milk to ship out every day. Rush Stuck was our milkman for many years. He would tell me many exciting things that I would never find out otherwise, plus a few wild stories! We milked about thirty cows when I came to the farm. I soon learned how to hold the milk bucket between my feet and fill it up. If a cat was close buy, I would shoot a stream of milk to her mouth, and also to mine. That is when you really got fresh milk to drink!

In the late forties Mother purchased a Surge milking system. We would hang a leather strap over the cows back, then we hung this vacuum machine on the strap. A hose and four teat cups would be fastened to her udder and this would draw the milk out.

It is amazing how much milk a cow can produce in one twelve hour period. Mother would keep about twenty-five Holstein cows and a few Guernsey or Jersey cows to give a better butter fat milk quality. A few years later, we changed from the Surge system to a pipeline milk and bulk tank. This ended the carrier track for cans and we got an electric barn cleaner that cleaned the stables, so I saw many changes on the farm.

Chapter 6

Lots of Fun on the Farm

There was a never-ending stream of water flowing through our farm. In the spring when the winter snows would melt, fish would come up the stream to spawn. I would lie on my belly, quickly reach under the eroded banks, and catch suckers. They were good to eat, but they were blessed with a lot of bones. Sometimes I would catch a nice trout, and of course, you might grab a water snake that you would let go of in a hurry. I never liked snakes. In the summer time when the water was low in the stream and, if I wanted to get a drink, I would get down on my belly again and suck the warm water up between my teeth. That way I would not get any minnows in my mouth since they were in the shallow pools too.

Sometimes I would set traps for muskrats. I caught a few, skinned them, and sold the hides. I also caught some opossums and once a skunk. Then I quit trapping. I must tell you about the skunk. I could not figure out how to get the skunk out of the trap without being sprayed. I finally thought if I got above the skunk with a wide pronged fork, I could pin it to the ground. Then I could release it. That seemed simple enough. I was unprepared for the next moment. When the fork hit the skunk on the back, there was a stream of odor on my fork and hands instantly. I went up to the house and washed my hands with tomato juice, which usually kills the skunk odor. After that, I forgot the trapping business!

I remember another of my business ventures when I was about fifteen. I would go into the woods to look for red root sassafras trees. There seemed to be a demand for tea made from the root of the sassafras tree. Now there are two kinds of sassafras trees. One is white and the other is red, so you made sure that you got the red, because the white was bitter. The only way to get it was to dig up the roots in the spring when the roots were full of sap. So, I made a deal with a man in Belleville who owned a grocery store. Russell Weyant owned the local Schaeffer's grocery store. He would pay me thirty-five cents for every little brown bag of dried tree root bark I gathered. I soon was digging up these red sassafras roots, peeling the bark off them, and drying them on the top of mother's heat radiators. Then I would bag it up and take it to the store. I was really making some money.

About this time, we went to Huntingdon one day. Mother said, "Now while we are in town, we will go to the bank and open a savings account for you." The name of the bank was The Grange Trust Company. Mother said we would sell a calf at the Belleville Livestock Market and the income from that would go into this new account. The calf sold for $21.00. That was my first experience with a bank.

We used to get very cold winters in the forties and fifties with lots of snow. The wind would blow the snow into deep drifts and the road would blow shut for days. I remember one time in the middle forties we got so much snow and then the wind began to blow. The state highway workers used to install snow fence that they set back from the road, and as the snow would come to it, the wind deposited that snow in drifts! The drifts got so high that we could walk to the country store about a quarter of a mile away and step over top of the telephone crossbars and insulators. The main roads were blown shut with the snow, and then the farmers and we older children would take big scoop shovels and shovel snow so that the highway snowplow could push the rest away. We would hitch up the horses to the big bobsled, then Sammie and I would go through the fields with the ten-gallon cans of milk to the Milk Plant in Belleville three miles away. Afterwards we would pick up feed at Roy Stuck's mill. One particular morning, the temperature was minus eighteen degrees when we walked to school. The snow would crunch under our boots. We all sat in the corner with the teacher beside the big stove and she would read us stories. Then we went home early because of the cold room.

Another experience I want to share is the time when Sammie and I would go to the woodland to cut trees down with our crosscut saw for lumber. Sammie taught me how to properly use the crosscut saw. He said, "You do not push the saw, but just pull it in proper sequence, and it will be so easy to saw a big log in half." It was not too long after that time that some men from Lewistown came to my mother and wanted to sell her this new thing called a chain saw. Well, Mother said, "If you can cut this great big white oak tree down that grows so close to the farm lane, then I will buy your saw." The tree was more than five feet across the stump, so the men took this big saw and cut sides off the tree to get the four-foot blade through the trunk. It was not long until the tree was on the ground! Therefore, Mother bought this two-man Mall chain saw with a four-foot blade and a little handle that would fit on the end of the blade. Now it

We are sitting on the giant oak tree that was just cut down with the new Mall chain saw. Seated left to right: Peg Mohler, Martha, George, Monroe, and Lizzie. Standing Harold Mohler, husband of Peg, and Sammie.

would take a strong man to handle that forty-nine pound saw, but as a youth, I did it lots of times.

One time as we were making hay I had a scare that I remember well. We had the tractor hooked up to the wagon and the hay loader hooked on the back. The loader would bring the dry hay up on the wagon and we would spread the hay around. Suddenly I saw a big black snake mixed in with the hay and as I was barefoot, it scared me badly. Sammie was on the wagon with me. He calmed me down, but I was very alert for snakes and thistles that would harm my feet.

We raised a lot of hogs, and I soon learned from the veterinarian how to dress little boar pigs so they would grow into better quality pigs. We would have to ring the large pigs so they would not tear up the ground so much. This meant we would tie the big pig to the wall in the pen and use a special tool to crimp a steel ring in the nose part of the hog. It usually took three rings to prevent them from rooting up the ground.

We had a big boar that I was afraid of. One day, Mother said, "We just have to ring that hog, but we must be careful because he has those big tusks sticking out the sides of his mouth."

Sammie and I took a strong chain, which we got it in his mouth behind those tusks, and we tied him to one of the oak posts along the pen. This made the boar very angry and he had a real hateful look in his eyes as we tightened the chain! We managed to get four rings in his snout, but I am sure if he could have gotten us cornered, he would have killed us. He did a lot of loud squealing and jerking around and I was sure glad when we were done.

My parents also raised peacocks on the farm

and sold them. Peacocks are exotic birds that grow beautiful long tails. One time a story about mother and her birds appeared in the Harrisburg paper called *The Patriot*. In the article, it showed a picture of my parents with her favorite bird called Pretty Bird. Did you know that peacocks make a very loud sound that can be heard a mile away?

My parents raised little dogs called toy terriers and Chihuahuas. Some of these little fully-grown dogs could fit in a large coffee cup. Mother would often carry them in her pocket-book around town with only the dog's head visible!

Our farmhouse had a large bell mounted on the top of the house roof. A large rope was fastened onto the bell and extended down through the attic, second floor, and first floor. There it was fastened to the wall

Monroe and Katie Mae in front of the hand carved fireplace mantel located in the big living room.

in the dining room. When Sammie and I would be far from the house, mother would ring the bell to call us for our meals. The sound carried for miles. Mother said the bell would be rung for an emergency if that would ever occur.

Katie Mae sitting in the winter dining room mending clothes.

In the late forties, mother was having trouble with arthritis in her hip. She found an electric elevator in a convent that was for sale. She hired the Otis Elevator Company from Harrisburg, Pennsylvania, to install it in her house. The elevator went from the basement up to the second floor, and it is still in use. Mother told us it cost her $1500 to buy the used elevator and $1500 to install it. By today's standards, it was very cheap. If you did not want to use the elevator, you could run up the winding hand carved stairway from the first floor to the attic!

Sammie standing beside the hand carved winding stairway from the first floor, past the second floor, up to the attic.

Once I had an experience with a snake that I will always remember. When I was maybe fourteen, mother told me to go out to this one line fence and cut all the brush and pile it up to burn. Later when the pile dried, I went out and made a big fire. A black snake crawled out. I took my fork, scooped up the snake, and threw it in the fire. When the snake hit the fire, it screamed like a hurt child! I was afraid! I thought the devil was in the snake and it was being killed with the snake. Now, I better understood the story in the Bible of the serpent who deceived Eve in the Garden of Eden, and how some people worshipped a snake on a pole. I will remember the sound that the snake made until I am dead!

Another time when I took Mother's 22 rifle out to the chicken house to shoot rats, there was a young cow that had developed an illness and she could not get up, so Sammie said we must call the veterinarian soon or she would die. We had her in the basement of the chicken house. Now about that time a rat ran across an opening and stopped to see what I was doing, I was quick enough to line up on that rat and pulled the trigger. That was the end for that rat, but, when the gun cracked, the cow stood right up and started to walk around. I decided that this cow must have been in a trance. I hurried up to the barn and told Sammie what happened; we still do not know how that loud gunshot sound affected her so.

I had a close call with death once. As we were unloading hay in the barn, I had just set the grapple hook in the load of hay. I motioned Mother, who was on the little Farmall Cub tractor, to start pulling the big hay rope, so that the load of hay would go straight up to the track and latch on to the dolly that would take it across the gable to the mow. As Mother began to lift the hay off the load, I discovered that my foot was caught in the trip rope and I was going with the hay to the top of the barn! I saw my life coming to an end. I worked frantically to free my foot, and just as I reached the top, I managed to trip the rope. Mother suddenly realized the slack in the rope and looked back just in time to see me falling back down on the wagon right on top of the loose hay! It was a scary experience. I was very fortunate to not have any broken bones; you can bet that I always checked the trip rope after that.

Mother and Dad made three ponds on the farm. One was in a limestone shale quarry, which Mother stocked with trout. The second one was along a shale bank and stocked with goldfish. The third one was about an acre or more in size and was located behind the barn. It was created for fire protection. Mother stocked it with bass and bluegills. The entire family had many good times fishing in the ponds, but so did herons, kingfishers, loons, snapping turtles, and other creatures. Mother got so mad at them. She told me to take the 22 rifle and shoot them, and I did. This improved my shooting abilities. Many a bird met its demise snitching fish from mother's ponds! One night a lot of nice big trout disappeared. I sincerely believe she thought that someone stole in and caught them. I later saw a mink around there, but I could not convince her that the mink ate them all.

In the late forties, my parents decided to build a cave in the little hill behind the house. We had a man take a backhoe and dig out a section sixteen feet by twenty feet and Monroe, Sammie, and I hauled limestone rocks in from old rock piles. We built the front from those stones with a door in the center. We used concrete for walls along the sides and in the back. Mother found a man near Lewistown that made his own curved wood rafters to form a curved roof. We borrowed those from him to make the roof for our cave. This was very exciting for me to see how Dad would make the top hold the heavy concrete.

We used many little trees from the woods to support the ceiling until the cement was hard. Then we covered the whole top and sides with dirt. All you could see was the front stone finish of the cave. I ran a wire underground from the basement to the cave for lights. This was my first electrical job. I was anxious to see if the light would come on when I tripped the switch, and it did! Mother wondered how

I knew how to do that. I was always ready to see how things worked. I would go to houses that were being built and study the framework, so I could do that myself some day. God had many plans for my life, and for me to be patient until those times came.

CHAPTER 7

New People

Mother had started a bed and breakfast business before I came to live there. It was so much fun for me to see the same guests come back year after year, especially those who remembered me! Now, you see there were a never-ending variety of people from all over the country who came to visit the farm. There was one special person who I dearly loved. Her name was Wilma. She is at the top of my list of people who loved me when I was small and she told me that she wished she would have found me before Katie did. Wilma, and her husband, Don, had three adopted children. They would come to Mother's in the summer with their three children giving me playmates!

*East view of my new home. Note the date 1836 on the plaque
located in the upper center of photo.*

Early in the summer, Mother would bring a woman
from the Lancaster area to stay all summer. Her
name was Annie May and she was a comical soul.
She loved all of us kids and would bring us candy
and spoil us. Another couple named Harry and Edna
Hawker from New Jersey, were annual visitors to the
farm. They had a car that the front doors opened
toward the front. Harry was hard of hearing, so we
had to talk louder. My young years may sound like a
mixture of people from many backgrounds, but that
is the way you learn.

Another woman lived in Huntingdon who owned
and operated a jewelry store. She would come to the
farm almost every weekend so she had her own special
bedroom. Her name was Blanche Black, and she was

Janie in front; second row, Anna Martha, George, and Annie May; third row, Katie Mae, Edna, and Harry Hawker, Sammie, and Monroe.

never married. She loved us children and would give us a ride to school in her 1936 brown Buick. All the children in school would come running to her car, because they knew she would give us candy.

One day my friend, Blanche Black, took me with her to Huntingdon to watch the trains. I said I wanted to be an engineer. She said she had a surprise for me. The East Broad Top train that went from Huntingdon way up the mountain to Robertsdale had come into the Huntingdon station. Blanche said she knew the engineer, so he got me to climb up into the locomotive and put me in the driver's seat. When I pulled the levers, the engine hissed with steam and we went forward. With a valve change, we went backward. That was a thrill of a lifetime for a young teenager.

Mother and another woman, named Becky Hooley, started the Goose Day tradition around 1942 in

Mifflin County. This is now celebrated the last week of September all over the Mifflin County area. Eating goose on Goose Day will bring you good luck and put you in a positive mood! I well remember visiting with Becky as she and Mother talked about this idea. We started raising geese and in the fall, we dressed them and took them to a few restaurants. This idea seemed to catch on because in the sixties, we raised more than seventy geese and Mother had other farmers in Big Valley raising geese for her orders. I went with her to the Elks Club, Honey Creek Inn, and a number of Lewistown restaurants. Mother was fussy about the geese we sold. All the pinfeathers and hair had to be picked off. She kept this work up until the middle seventies when she had a stroke. Then her friends took this project over.

There was a man named Kenneth Eungard who was the dealer for John Deere farm equipment in Center County. It was always exciting for me to see him coming up our lane with a new John Deere tractor, hay rake, disk plow, corn picker, or new farm wagon.

As I was out working in the fields on the tractor, I would often sing as loudly as I could. People told me later that they could not see who was driving the tractor, but they recognized my voice. I still love to sing, praising the Lord.

Mother was a widow from 1939 until 1945, as I said before. She would go to Sarasota, Florida, in the wintertime. One day in the spring of 1946, a man from the Lancaster County area came to the farm and said he was going to marry my mother. It turned out he had met Mother in Pinecraft, a suburb of Sarasota, Florida, and he was a widower with eight sons to his first wife. They were all grownup and married. One son was killed in World War II and is buried in Germany. Monroe Mohler was sixty-six years old, twenty years older than mother. They were married in Maryland on December 18, 1946. (As of this writing, there are three of my half brothers still living: Jack, Clarence, and Bill. Martin, Galen, Ralph, Harold, and Aaron are deceased. We have a Mohler reunion each year, so we maintain a great relationship with each other.)

Monroe's seven sons and I. Front row, left to right: Martin, Galen, and Ralph. Back row, left to right: George, Bill, Harold, Clarence, and Jack.

Monroe was a very smart man. He knew so much about many things, and since he was born in 1880, he had lots of stories to tell. He taught us children to love and respect our neighbors and to be responsible for our own actions. He was also a calming influence on Mother when she got upset and angry. However, sometimes he would get in the truck and drive to Belleville to think things over and get away from her for a while. One day as Monroe was washing the car, mother came out to him, and he turned the garden hose on her. That was an exciting moment as she hurried away.

When I was fourteen, I decided to be baptized in the new Allensville Mennonite Church. The church was built in 1949, so I remember when Bishop Raymond Peachey and Reverend Elrose Hartzler baptized me. It was a very humbling experience for me because I wanted to be a part of the family of God. When you accept Christ as your savior from sin, you develop spiritual growing pains. I felt frustrated, wondering why my mother would do some of the shady things that she did. I would have to take the blame for things that happened between my sisters and me.

One day I felt so frustrated that I took a piece of paper and listed all of the things I was blamed for, that I did not do and placed the paper where Mother would later find it. The next day she called me into the house and when I saw her, she was holding the paper. Thus began an investigation of things, but I stood my ground. From that day on my sister was double-checked to see who really was the instigator!

My mother would serve meals to private parties in our house. We had two large rooms where we could seat many people; the smallest group we ever served was thirteen, and the largest was seventy-two. There was a partition between these rooms on a track that would slide in to the end wall. This way we could set several long tables end to end. A lot of time was spent on food preparation, making pies and homemade ice cream and black walnut cakes, plus all the seven sweets and seven sours and everything in between! Mother always wanted me to help serve the meals and I loved it. Before we would eat, she would have me stand at the corner of the table and say a prayer. It had to be right from the heart and not written on paper.

Mother was noted for her ability to do things that few other folks could do! During war times, many things were rationed including sugar, but Mother managed to get five hundred pounds in 100 pound bags. When she came home, she told me to put it on the kitchen table in the storage room so the mice could not get to it. Later on someone asked her how she got so much sugar and she told them, "I don't know what you are talking about because all the sugar I have is on the kitchen table!" So reader, look between the lines. Of course, she needed it to continue baking!

Mother was the kind of person that if she needed

Katie Mae and her friend Elsie Noe. Elsie's husband, Ralph, took the picture that is on the cover of this book.

Katie Mae on the John Deere tractor mowing the field.

something from the government she would drive right to Harrisburg and go into the capital building or other building and tell them what she wanted and she would get results before she left the place! Therefore, I may have learned some ways to get results from higher ups, but I would not do some of the things that she did!

CHAPTER 8

The Other Farm

My mother owned another farm about a mile from our home farm. There was a nice two-story house on it that they rented. When I came to Mother's in 1941, there were people living there named Price who had several children. Mother said that they had a hard time surviving and she would rent it to them very cheaply if they would help with the chores.

Mr. Price lived there several years and their children went to the same school that I did. After they moved away, Sammie and Mother tilled the fields and I drove the tractor to do the easy work. We kept a lot of young cattle in the barn in the winter and pastured them through the summer.

I have a few memories of events on this farm that are worth telling.

There were several cherry trees along the fencerow. One day as we were picking cherries off of a high tree, we set the wooden ladder up to reach the top. Mother was standing on the back of the truck and Lizzie went up the ladder to pick those high branches. I suddenly heard this thump and I quickly realized that Lizzie had fallen down! I knew that Lizzie was at least 20 or more feet above the ground. When she fell, she slid along the ladder down on to the thick grass.

Mother got all excited and told me to come down out of the tree and help her with Lizzie. Mother tried to take her pulse and she finally said that she believed that Lizzie just passed out. I put some water on her face, and she came back to life! I was so glad to see that because I first believed that she had died! She soon recovered from that fall with no broken bones, but Mother said that Lizzie should stay off the ladder from that time on.

My parents said that we needed a new water line installed from the mountain down across the fields to this farm. She knew of an old man by the name of Roll Zook who lived in Allensville. He liked to dig in the ground with a pick and shovel. He told her he would dig the ditch for her if she would come get him in the morning and make his meals.

There was over 2000 feet of ditch to dig and Mother told him to make it three feet deep and a foot wide. She took the tractor with a single bottom plow and made one pass down through the field. This gave him a straight line almost a foot deep to start digging.

Meanwhile my father and I began to build a little reservoir up stream. By the time Mr. Zook had dug the ditch, we were done with the little dam and the valves. Sammie and I got 3\4 inch galvanized pipe and put it in the ditch and mother pushed the ditch shut with the snow plow that we had mounted on the tractor. It was exciting for me to see the water coming out of the water spigot at the barn when we were all done.

One time, hornets built a large nest twelve feet above the ground in the pear tree that was near the farmhouse. Mother and I got stung and my eye swelled shut, so mother said we would fix them! Two nights later after dark, mother drove the truck under the tree, and then Sammie and I quickly put a big burlap bag over the nest, sawed the branch off, and tied it shut! The hornets got very mad and I was so afraid that they would come through that bag. Mother drove the truck home with Sammie and me on the back. She stopped at the creek and told us to put that bag down in the deep water hole and put a big rock on top of it, and we did! The next day I looked and there were no more hornets around.

Since we farmed all those fields, I would drive the tractors back and forth a lot. One day as I was driving the John Deere with the spreader hitched on, I went over a bump and the hitch pin fell out. The spreader went over in the neighbor's field. Luckily, there was no damage done to the spreader, and I got it hooked back up before anyone came around. I know I would have gotten the dickens if Mother had found out.

We put long days in those fields. Once as I was driving the tractor home late in the evening, I got so sleepy, I drifted off of the road and into the neighbor's fence. I heard a loud screech and I got awake very quickly and stopped the tractor. I was lucky again because no one ever said anything about that.

One day my nephew Jacob Zook said he wanted me to go with him to the woods to check on a few things. When we got there, he told me to stay by this tree until he came back. About a half hour later, I heard this terrible howling noise coming from the direction that he had gone. I thought that a lion or bear was killing him and soon the animal would find and kill me too. I was only 9 years old, but I climbed that tree very quickly. After a short time Jacob came and he asked what I was doing up in the tree? I told him that I heard this terrible noise and I was very much afraid that a bear or lion would get me; he said that he did not hear anything. A year or so later, someone asked me if I was scared and afraid the day that Jake took me along with him to the woods and made those wild sounds just to scare me. I guess he got his thrill, but I decided to keep my distance from him.

One day as Sammie and I were fixing the fence along the woods, I looked down on a section of bare ground. Right in the middle of the ground laid a gray Indian arrowhead. Boy, was I excited. I still have that arrowhead.

Another time, Sammie and I found a very old turtle. Someone had carved a date on the bottom. It was marked 1911 with the initials J.S. Box turtles live a very long time, because we found that one around 1952.

Sammie and I would go from home to the other farm several times a week to feed the young cattle during the winter months. One day in the early spring, as we passed this one field, I saw this pink colored balloon near the far end of the field. I told Sammie that it was not there the other day and could I go and see what it was. He said I could, so I hurried to see what it was. There I found a wooden box about the size of a large cereal box fastened to a torn balloon! A note on the box stated it was a weather-testing unit that was released at Pittsburgh the day before. The note requested that the finder please return it to the address found on the box. Sammie and I were delighted to find this treasure, so we took it to the Post Office. Soon after that, we received a thank you note from the weather service. I kept the torn balloon for many years as a memory.

One fall day Sammie and I were picking corn in one of the fields near where Andy Byler now lives. Sammie drove the tractor and I was on the wagon when I noticed this big rabbit run out of the cornfield. As it ran into the woods, I saw it take a somersault and then I did not see it anymore. I got off of the wagon and went over to where I had last seen it. I realized then that the rabbit, in its haste to get away, ran right into the face of a big rock and died of a crushed skull. I took that rabbit home, cleaned it, and Lizzie fried it for a meal.

One problem we had on the farm that got mother upset was a dog from the town of White Hall which came down to our farm frequently. We would catch it sometimes and mother would give it a good licking and it would dash over across the fields to its home.

Days later the dog came back, so mother said she would give that dog a lesson it would not forget. We caught the dog and she tied a piece of strong chord to its tail. Then she threaded the chord through several empty tin cans, tied a knot in the last can, and left the dog loose. We stood there and laughed so hard as the dog ran down the lane. Soon the dog got stuck in the fence, but got loose when we tried to free it. Then it ran up to its home. It really made a loud noise when it ran up on the blacktop road. It was very funny to us at the time, but it was not very funny to the dog's owner. A few days later mother got a call from White Hall. The caller did not identify himself, but said there was a dead German Shepard dog laying in the neighbor's yard, and he thought it was hers. Sammie took the truck, and got the dead dog. It was ours, and Mother realized it must be payback time. The dog had been shot.

CHAPTER 9

The Sixteen and Older Years

Father taught me how to drive and he took me for my driver's test. I was so sure I would pass, but I had to go the second time. When I turned eighteen he took me to see Urie Zook, the man from our church that was the contact person for the government as far as military service was concerned. My parents filled out the forms stating that they needed me on the farm to work, so I did not have to serve in the military or do voluntary service either. I do not think that there were any wars going on then.

My sister Anna Martha and I had many wonderful times together. However, sometimes we would fight and argue. One day Anna Martha did something against me. It had to be discussed at the dinner table like usual. Then Mother said, "You take her down to the basement and give her a good licking." So, down the steps we went.

I told her, "I cannot lick you because you are my sister, so when I hit the wall with the stick you holler 'ouch'." She did so several times and I said, "Now rub your eyes because you must look like you are crying when we go back upstairs." Mother never knew the difference.

I think the worst thing that happened to me was losing my sister from our home, as I will explain. Anna Martha struggled with her arithmetic. She had to stay home one morning from school and study her lessons. Later Mother told Dad to take her to school and leave her there. Anna Martha thought that Mother did not want her anymore, so Martha did not get on the bus to come home. She went down to Lester Zook's store with her friend to get a sandwich. She said she wanted to get her haircut and go the modern way! Now when the time came to sit down at the supper table to eat, Mother said, "Where's Anna Martha?" Mother looked straight at me and said, "Do you know where she is?"

Of course, I knew, but I wanted to protect Anna Martha, and I knew that if I did not tell it all, she would find out later. Dad was looking at me and I knew I would get a terrible licking, so I told them that she did not like it here anymore. She did not want to come home so she ran away to her friend's house in Allensville. I never saw Mother move so fast as when she rose from the table. She and Dad left quickly in the truck to go to Allensville and found her at the store. It was not long until they came up our lane with her. Soon they were back sitting at the supper table. Janie and I were very upset. Just when Mother and Anna Martha sat down, Anna Martha reached into the drawer for something that she mistook for sugar. It turned out to be strychnine poison, which she put into her mouth. Mother hurried her to the sink to wash her mouth out. This was all very painful for me. There seemed to be a lot of friction between them.

Anna Martha was not allowed to go with me to youth meetings at church. I told Mother that she would not have wanted anyone to tell her what to do when she was young, so she should allow Anna Martha to have enjoyment with other young people her age, too. Mother got mad at me for taking Anna Martha's side.

Things got worse from that time on. Anna Martha had just turned seventeen and Mother was responsible for her until her eighteenth birthday. One day Mother called me upstairs in the little hallway and there stood Lizzie, Anna Martha, and Dad. I saw that Anna Martha was crying, and I thought to myself, "Now what?"

Mother said, "I have had it with her! Soon she will be eighteen and I am only responsible for her until then. So tomorrow Dad and I are going to take her back to the orphanage where we got her," which she did the next day. That ended a fourteen-year growing up together time for us.

I liked Anna Martha, and I wanted to run off too. I thought I would take some clothes and slip over the mountain to Mattawanna where the trains went and jump on a train to some-where, but I did not. I cried a lot about that experience and I am crying now as I write this. It was a turning point in Anna Martha's life that did her no good.

Many years later, I met the pastor of the Masontown Mennonite Church, who was formerly from the Big Valley area. He knew some of our history and told me that Anna Martha had attended his church for a while. He thought she might still be in that area. When he went back to his church, he contacted her and told her he had talked with George, who would love to see her!

Since Mother had passed away by this time, there was no holding us back. A short time later, my wife, Sammie, Lizzie, and I went to Masontown and visited Anna Martha. We had a wonderful time! Thirty years had passed since we had seen each other. Anna Martha got married, had three sons, and is now a grandmother. Her oldest son was found dead in his car one day and the second one was killed in a car wreck, so Anna Martha has had her share of sorrows and it was very necessary for us to get together to reminisce.

Martha Lindeman and her three sons. Left to right: Dwayne, Tom, Dale, and Martha. Her husband, Harold, passed away in 1971.

CHAPTER 10

Chasing Girls

My mother purchased an almost new Henry J. car for me on my eighteenth birthday. The

My 1953 Henry J car, made by the Kaiser Corp.

Kaiser Corporation made this car. It was light blue and I wish I still had it. It would be worth a lot of money now! I felt that I was left out of a cage. At last, I had wheels and I could go visit my buddies and start chasing girls.

In my late teens, I felt that I needed to get out with other young people so I decided to get involved with the Mennonite Youth Fellowship (MYF) at the Maple Grove Mennonite Church. Mother did not mind too much except the chores had to be done first. I thought she seemed to find things for me to do that would delay my game plan.

At that time, I met Loren Glick, who was the son of Mr. and Mrs. Elam Glick. We ran around together for a couple of years and he was special to me. Sorry to say, one day as he was driving the farm tractor across the little bridge near his barn, the tractor slipped off the bridge and upset, killing him. That was a terrible shock to me. We confided in each other and were good friends. In addition, he knew more about girls than I did. I was very bashful at times, so to ask a girl to go out with me took real courage.

I finally decided I had to talk to this blond haired girl who lived near Milroy and came to MYF regularly. One Sunday afternoon, I started to drive in her long lane. I suddenly got nervous, put the car in reverse, and backed out the lane again! I still idolized her when she came to the meetings. I happened to see her about twenty-eight years after that and I told her about the possible date that never happened. We had a good laugh over that. Our meetings were usually held at John Mc Yoder's or at Esther Hostetler's homes. These leaders were a great blessing to me and my spiritual life was changed through them.

The Mennonite churches in our valley would sponsor a winter Bible School for adults. Sammie and I would try to go as much as possible because it only lasted for two weeks in January. In the winter of 1955, it was held at the Locust Grove Mennonite Church. At Bible School, we would get an in-depth study of God's word. The lessons would start at 9:00 a.m. and then break at noontime for a meal served in the basement by the women of the church. It was at one of these noon meals that a young woman sat across the table from me. I was sitting beside my friend, John Renno, and I asked him in a low voice, "Do you know who that pretty girl with blue eyes and brown hair is that is sitting across the table from me?"

He told me in a hushed tone, "Why she is Sam S. Yoder's daughter, Katie!"

I suddenly had heat waves go up my back and I said to myself—is this love at first sight? Now as I look back in time, I really believe God was showing me this girl and had planned for her to be my wife

Katie and her sister Amanda, when they were single. Katie is on the right.

someday. I found out where she lived and later drove my car to her house and we started dating.

After enjoying each other's company for several months, she said that she and her friend, Ruth Yoder, were going on a train to Iowa City, Iowa, to work in a crippled children's hospital for one year as volunteer workers through the Mennonite Churches Alternate Service Program. So, I said goodbye to her at the train station in Lewistown. This happened in the early summer of 1955.

We wrote back and forth for several months. One day I got a letter from her saying, maybe we should stop writing for a while to think things over. I called her long distance and said I really loved her and I wanted her to please keep on writing, and she did!

Halfway during their year of work, she and Ruth came home for the holidays. I was at the station to greet her and we got to talk a lot over Christmas. Soon they had to get back on the train and return to Iowa City. The next day we got word that, their train wrecked in Indiana and she suffered a bruised knee, which still bothers her a little now and then. It could have been a lot worse because some of the cars tipped off the tracks and some caught fire. I was very glad that she and Ruth came through the experience alive.

Katie finished her term in the spring of 1956 and we decided to get married on September 15 of that year. I did not ask my foster mother if it was okay with her since I was twenty-one. One Sunday morning as Mother and I were going to church I said that Katie and I planned to get married in September. I think she just about had the shock of her life! She said, "Pooh, that will fall through. I can tell you things about that family that you would be very sorry if you married her!" I felt rebuffed and I said we really did want to get married. She was at a loss for words.

(Let me share something the readers of this book need to know. My foster mother always wanted to be in control of every thing, even her husband and children. Sammie told me later that she was the same with him. He said that he had a great relationship with a girl in his dating days when he owned a horse and buggy. Mother told him that he would not be mentally able to take care of a woman like you should and that he was dumb in many things. He told me that if you are told all the time that you are dumb, you eventually become dumb. So you see, my mother was not always respected in the community like she could have been. Many times she would go out of the area to buy cars and farm equipment far from home because the local dealers were not good enough for her, except when she needed quick repair service. Then she expected them to fix it right away, and they told her to go to the place where she bought it!)

So to finish up this chapter, I want to say that my soon-to-be wife was the only girl that I really dated. I did some looking at other women, but no dating.

CHAPTER 11

Our Wedding and Beyond

The summer of 1956 passed rather quickly as
we made our wedding plans. My mother said I
should take the money that I had put in the bank
years before to buy a new suit and whatever else I
needed. She said she would make a nice wedding
dinner for us. We started inviting all of our friends
and my future wife's relatives, plus many people
in our churches. Mother had many friends that we
got to know over the years and we had over 300
people at our wedding. It was held at the Maple
Grove Mennonite Church, which I and a lot of other
volunteer workers helped to build in the winter of
1955-56. Bishop Aaron Mast performed the ceremony

and then we went to the Belleville Community Hall for the wedding reception.

Katie and I on our wedding day, September 15, 1956. Seated, left to right: Jewel Kauffman, her mother Amanda, my brother Bob Kloepfer as best man, and Ruth Yoder as maid of honor.

As Mennonite people, we did not have alcoholic drinks, but we had just about everything else, including roast pheasant, served with other meats, mashed potatoes, vegetables, salads, desserts, cake, and ice cream! We wanted to have a photographer, but Mother said that it would cost too much and a lot of people would take pictures and give us some of them anyway. We only got five or six photos of the wedding given to us later and that was all. We still had to follow Mother's laws.

My wife's sister had a cute little girl named Jewel who had red hair, and we had her sit at our table. The people that raised my biological sister and brother brought them to our wedding. After they left, we did not get to see them for eleven years. My mother did not want me to have a constant relationship with them. Like I said before, Mother had to have the last word in everything.

My new wife had one sister Amanda, and two brothers named Urie and Andy. I must say that Amanda's husband did not come to our wedding because he felt a lot about me like my mother felt about my wife. He had told my wife that she should not marry me because I would never amount to much. He said, "If you do, you will always be sorry!" As I think back over these things, I did not hold it against him that he said these things. Soon after, when he saw how successful I was, he came to visit us and eat at our table. How people change.

After our reception, Katie and I left for Niagara Falls on our honeymoon. It was a beautiful day for our wedding but later that night it began to rain so hard that we stopped at Renovo, Pennsylvania, for Saturday night. We felt exhausted after all of the wedding preparations, ceremony, and clean up after the reception.

Sunday morning we drove north on route 144 through the towns of Cross Forks, Germania, and Galeton and north into New York State, to the falls, and into Canada. Mother had arranged for us to stay at a tourist home on the Canadian side of the falls. We took in many of the attractions, riding on the Maid of the Mist boat and walking into the Cave of the Winds. We saw lots of other newlyweds too.

On Monday evening, the phone rang in our room and it was Mother. She said, "When are you coming home?" I said maybe Thursday, and then she said, "You must come home on Tuesday. We had a heavy frost and we must get ready to fill the silo with frosted corn!" So, Tuesday morning we left to come home.

My wife soon developed a strained relationship with my foster mother because she was nowhere to be found when we got home. Before Tuesday was over, Sammie and I had the silo pipes up and were ready to start filling the silo by Wednesday morning.

We lived in the grandfather end of the big house, where we had it fixed up very nice. Mother said we could have a quarter of beef, a whole hog, some eggs, and milk. She also said we only needed to go to the grocery store twice a month. She paid us $75 a month for my wages. We purchased a used refrigerator and a freezer. We received many nice gifts at our wedding so we were blessed. It is sad to say my wife and I cried a lot over Mother being so bossy, plus Katie soon became pregnant! In addition, to shake things up, one day the chimney caught fire and that scared Katie. We cooked and heated our end of the house with a cook stove, so we had lots of wood stored up. Some times the chimney would soot up and we had to watch that.

One morning in April, 1957 my wife said, "Honey, I do not want to stay here. Since your mother is in Florida, I want to move away from here before she comes home. My brother-in-law has an empty apartment in Rockville and he would let us rent that."

Now I had to make a decision. Do I move to Rockville and go back and forth to milk cows or say good-bye to the farm after sixteen years and get a job in the local factory? I was so sick and tired of getting up early every morning, being told all summer which tractor to use, which fields to work in, and which cow to dry up, plus a whole lot of other stuff. It seemed I could never have any say in the planning!

I also realized that Sammie and Lizzie would have all the work to do. Janie would go along with Mother and Father to Florida, so if I left the farm they would be stuck with the work, and they were not young themselves any more. After much thought we decided to move. We took the John Deere tractor and farm wagon and put all our belongings on it and we moved to the little town of Rockville about two miles away. Yost and Lomie Byler, Katie's half-sister and brother-in-law, owned the apartment. It was a cozy place. When Mother and Father came home from the South, they were not too happy about our moving. However, they realized that I was not going to be a farmer all my life, plus Mother was now 57 and Father was 77 years old. So, my mother called her friend Yonie Glick, who was a cattle dealer, and he came and bought the cows. Mother still kept some of the heifers, pigs, and chickens. It was a great change for all of us.

When Mother married Monroe Mohler, I took his name as my last name. However, I was not legally adopted. So when I got married, I had to use my birth name, Goerge Arthur Kloepfer. A friend suggested that I legally change my name before I had any children. I went to the judge at the courthouse in Lewistown, where a hearing was scheduled. Since no one contested my name change, I became George Kloepfer Mohler. This cost me a grand total of $300.

Ten months after our wedding, our daughter, Nancy Ann, was born at the hospital in Huntingdon. She was a big baby, weighing 9 lbs. 6 ounces. Katie had a hard time birthing her, she had to be turned. She was a beautiful baby! My wife said that her mother told her that having a baby was just like having one foot in the grave and many a mother met that fateful end.

I am very glad that God showed me this woman in Bible School and that I married her. She was very patient and we now had a wonderful child to love and cherish.

Our daughter, Nancy Ann, born June 26, 1957.

CHAPTER 12

No More Farm Work

I began working right away for Metz Hatchery, cleaning chicken houses, gathering eggs, and doing other maintenance work. I worked there from May 1, 1957, until the fall of 1958, when I got a job with the Pennsylvania Department of Highways. I enjoyed that job and made good money, so I decided to buy a brand new 1957 two-door hardtop Plymouth from John D. Grove and Son in Huntingdon, Pa. I paid $1,800 for that car.

Now this was a fast car! I could go 80 miles an hour in second gear. Many times I would go 120 miles an hour. One time my friend, who had a 1957 Chevy, wanted to race me. We went to a place in our valley that had a straight stretch of road. Now since we did not see anything coming in the opposite lane I got beside him and we took off as fast as we could go. He slowly pulled away from me until we got to 95—100 miles an hour, then I passed him. By then, I had to hit the brakes because we were running out of road visibility. As I look back at my fast car, it is a wonder that I am still alive.

I would travel down the valley in the mornings to work in Reedsville when I was employed by the state. One day I decided to pass a police officer that was going rather slow. When he was out of my sight, I floored it. When I got down to the stop sign in Reedsville, there was a long line of cars poking along and I could not pull out of the intersection quick like I wanted to. I heard this screeching noise beside me and when I looked in my rear view mirror, this police officer had accidentally straddled the concrete barrier trying to catch up with me. He said, "Hold it right there!" I saw right away that he was very angry. He yelled, "I almost killed myself trying to catch you," and, at the moment, I thought I wish he would have!

I followed him over to the justice of the peace located on Walnut Street and paid $35 for the fine. That was a lot of money back in the late fifties.

This fast life gradually got me into trouble that I did not expect. Many of the people that worked on the highway were beer drinkers. They thought I just had to go with them after working hours and have a few beers too. The men said I should try smoking, so one day they gave me some cigarettes to try, I did not like the idea, but I will try to see how it feels. A day or so I tried it again, the men said take a big draw of it and then blow it out your nose. There was a telephone pole close by and I reached for it, because I felt I would pass out. I said this is it, if that is what it does to you, it is not for me. I tell many young people that it is very uncool to smoke, but they just do not see it the way I do. Some day they will carry a small tank of oxygen with them, because their lungs are not able to work properly.

Now this was a new world of excitement for me, and I met quite a few wild women. After a few drinks, they start to look inviting. You start to dance and kiss and one thing leads to another, then you have to lie to your wife and stay out late. One night the men had to drive me home, because they were mixing drinks on me and I passed out. When they got me to my house and helped me into the kitchen, my wife told me, "One more night like that and you will have no wife!"

One day as we were working in Reedsville, a police officer stopped and talked to me for a while. He said that he had to take me into the police station to answer some questions. While I was there, they explained to me that I must be responsible for my actions or go to jail! Later as I stood before the judge, my church friends came to support me and helped me get back on the right track. I finally realized you cannot follow two paths through life. Sin thrills and sin kills. All those years of Bible study, prayer, and singing will not save you if you reject them like I almost did! I want to thank my good wife for staying by me during that short period. It has been said that in your young years, you sow your wild oats and when you suddenly come to your senses, you quickly pray for a crop failure! I made an absolute change in my life and switched jobs.

In the spring of 1959, we moved from Rockville to a larger house in White Hall owned by Ruth Zook, which was close to the farm where I used to live. Later I purchased an acre of land along the Back Mountain Road and began to build a two-car garage. We wanted to get into a place of our own as soon as possible. Sammie helped me build it and we moved in the fall of 1962. Now we had a little place of our own even though it was just a two-car garage with a well and sewer system. I made plans to eventually build a nice big ranch type house next to the garage. We took baths in a big round galvanized tub. We had a lot of fun in that little 24×24 garage.

I went to work for J.M. Young and Sons in Belleville. It was the best decision I made in my young years. I met an older man who worked at this company, and he became like a mentor to me. As we worked together, I learned a lot about building. I was soon put in charge of the roofing and siding crews. I just loved the company, and they appreciated me. I worked for them for over five years.

In 1960, I decided to learn to fly. I found out that the local airport staff had just hired a flying instructor. The airport was close to home and my friend was planning to take lessons too. We got together and decided to travel back and forth together. We each put in enough hours with the instructor that we could soon fly the little airplane by ourselves!

One day my wife said to me, "Honey, I really am afraid to fly in that little airplane and I wish you would quit before something happens to you." Therefore, I eventually gave up flying.

In the summer of 1960, my friend Leonard Roth
and I were riding his motorcycle from the airport up
our valley, when I saw a big cloud of smoke far ahead.
I thought that a house or barn must be on fire.

We soon covered six miles until we got to the fire
and I saw right away that mother's barn was burning!
I hurried down to the house and asked Sammie what
in the world happened? He said that he was in the hog
pen and he just looked over at the barn floor, when
he saw this flame of fire beginning to go up along the
hay mow. He hurried to the house and called the fire
company. They came in a hurry, but it burned too
fast. He managed to get the young cattle out but the
big bull died of smoke inhalation in his pen.

A lot of memories of times spent in the barn milking
cows, pulling up hay and a lot of carpenter work that
I did, went up in smoke. Mother went to Lancaster
and found a man that built barns the old fashioned
way using the mortise and tendon method of tying
logs and beams together with wooden pins.

Aaron Lapp came and stayed at mother's house
for several weeks, and he had some men with him to
measure and notch the timbers. Sammie and I went
to the woods and cut a number of nice oak trees, and
took them to the sawmill. When all the logs were cut
and measured to exact lengths we had a barn raising
and lots of men came to build it, but it was not the
same as the original.

A few weeks after the new barn was finished, Mother
and I were discussing the barn fire. She said to me,
"George, you didn't light the barn on fire did you?"

I said, "Why do you say a thing like that?" She
went on to say that her friends in Iowa, who had also

taken children to raise, had a bad experience with one of the children. One of their girls became very mad and lit their barn on fire! I guess this is what possessed mother to ask me this question.

I was very glad that I had a perfect excuse. I told her that Leonard Roth and I were coming back from a pilot training lesson when we saw the fire. I hurt inside for a long time that she would even think to ask me a question like that, but that was the way mother acted at times.

In May of 1963, my mother called me saying that some of her friends from Ohio were in visiting and they would like to meet us as they had heard a lot about my abilities to do many things, so after supper we went to visit mother and her friends. There we met Mr. and Mrs. Chester Campbell.

We had a great conversation with them and he asked me if we would like to come and visit them sometime soon. I had never been to Ohio before and the idea seemed great for a vacation. We decided to go there some time but not that year.

I joined the Big Valley Men's Chorus and we sang at many different churches. I liked to sing the tenor part, we had a quartet, too. I also sang in a choir at Maple Grove Mennonite church. We had a radio program on the local radio station, and I was a part of that. I also led music at our church services.

CHAPTER 13

We Move to Ohio

In April of 1964, Mr. Campbell called me from Ohio and said that he needed a man like me to do specialty work. Would I please come out and look the place over? Two weeks later Mother, Father, Katie, Nancy, and I went to Ohio. I had never been west of Pittsburgh, so we were in new country. As Mr. Campbell showed us around his company layout, we felt this was what God wanted us to do. I handed a two-week notice to my employer and said that we were moving to Ohio. Mr. Young said he did not like the idea, but he could not hold me back. We decided to move on Memorial Day of 1964.

When we got to Massillon, Mr. Campbell had a

nice house rented for us, and he helped us move our belongings inside. We realized at the end of the day, that we left our house in the morning in Belleville and at the end of the same day we were now in a house located on Crystal Lake Avenue near Canal Fulton, Ohio.

Katie, Nancy, and George, taken when we lived in Ohio.

On Monday morning, I went to work for Mr. Campbell, or "Chet" as he was called. He introduced me to his employees, we toured the buildings, he gave me a Chevy work van to use, and I soon had all my equipment in it. I realized that I was where God wanted me to be.

The owner of the house we rented invited us to come to the church he attended, the Amherst Community Church, which was only a mile or so away from the house where we lived. We just loved it. We were soon involved in the church and became Sunday school teachers. We were asked if we would be janitors and

I was soon serving on the church board. We had a lot to learn because we had come from a conservative area and we did not know about going out to a restaurant for steaks and baked potatoes, and many other things.

I remember times when our church had a softball team and we would go and play against other church teams. One of the highlights of our church that was so special to me was when we started a Bible quiz team. This group of teenagers would get together in the basement of our home and study a book of the Bible for a few months. When we felt that our team of eight teenagers felt good about their accomplishments, we would go to another church that had a Bible quiz team and compete against them.

We had a set of electric switches mounted on five chairs all linked together. When a student felt that he knew the answer to a question, he would jump off his chair, and a light would show which person jumped up from the chair first! We developed a lot of key questions from the book in the Bible that we had studied. When the time came to quiz, a twenty-question sheet was made up to ask the team. Tom Harper was the captain and I was co-captain, and we made up the questions to be asked and the team did not see the questions ahead of time. We had two sets of twin boys and four girls, including our daughter, on the team. We would pick the ones that we felt comfortable with at each quizzing period. Our team tried to be the very best they could and we won the Ohio State Bible quiz matches! We went to Ontario, Canada and won a contest there.

We made plans to go to Los Angeles, California to

compete in the national finals. There we faced some real challenges, but we made it to the top team. As we finished the twentieth question, the opposing team felt that we did not answer the last question properly because our competitor said, "Is that all?" The other team said that she should not have added those three words to the answer. They claimed that she did not know all of the answer, which was not the case at all. After much deliberation, the judges ruled in their favor and we went home very sad because we knew that we were right. Later the judges said that they realized they had made a bad judgment call, but it was too late to change.

I was invited to join the Jackson Township Lions Club. I felt I was not worthy, but they said it was not how much money you had but what is in your heart when it comes to helping your fellow man. I have been a Lions Club member for over 40 years now and still love it. I am presently the president of our club.

Our daughter, Nancy, began her second year of school at Jackson Elementary School. We lived in a high-class area so things cost more than back home, and my wages were just double what they were in Pennsylvania. Six months after we moved from Belleville, we decided to sell our little two-car garage in Pennsylvania and take that money to buy a nice ranch type house near the church on Beatty Street. This was a good investment as we later realized.

I really enjoyed working with the seventeen employees in the company. Chet invited me into his inner circle of friends and we did things together with his millionaire buddies that the other workers never did. At Christmas, Chet distributed ten percent of the year's profits to all the employees according to their seniority. I serviced oil burners, set gas pumps, delivered oils and all kinds of things, even poured concrete for new stations. One thing I did not do was mechanical work; he had his regular men do that. Chet purchased a farm, too. He wanted me to help him fix things up so he could hire a farmer to till the fields and milk cows. Chet was a millionaire, but he did not let it go to his head. He became like a father to me. We spent a lot of time on that farm. I installed a barn cleaner and I concreted the whole big barnyard. I covered half of the barn with new boards and I built over a half mile of woven wire fence. Chet asked, "How did you get it so straight?" He was proud of my work and was always bragging about me. I told him it just came naturally.

He would buy expensive tickets to shows and football games. He would rent a large bus to come to his house to take all his wealthy friends to a football game; and, of course, I had to be on that bus. Much could be said about the oil company and the things that Mr. Campbell did for the community. God really blessed his work and he thanked the Lord for that.

One day I said to Chet, "I have worked almost seven years for you and we had a most memorable time together. Now my foster parents are getting up in years and they need me. Katie is homesick and we need to move back to Pennsylvania. Our daughter will be entering high school and we need to make the change now."

Then he said, "I felt it would come to this and I want you to do what you think is best for your family, but I think you would be making a big financial mistake. I understand your situation and I realize you and I had a great time together so you do what you think is best."

I did not want him to be upset with me for leaving the company, so I said, "Chet, when I leave this place I want to go in peace and happiness." I thought about this for a month or so and I mentioned to the workers at the plant that I wanted to sell my house and move back to Pennsylvania. Very soon after that, one of the men said that his daughter was moving back to Massillon and was looking for a house. They soon came to look at our house and said it was just what they were looking for; so, they bought it for the price we were asking.

In November of 1969, we were traveling from Massillon, Ohio, to Belleville, to hunt deer. The weather was warm and rainy. As we approached the town of Allensville, the road appeared to have a foamy surface. Suddenly the car began to slide to the right on to the berm, I got it straightened out when it slid across to the left lane and back to the right and back to the left where it went up the bank at an angle and rolled over on the top. We slid across the road, hit the bank, and spun around. The roof was smashed down against the top of the front seat where my wife's head should have been. I did not have my seat belt on but Katie did. To this day, I cannot figure out how she got her head under the dashboard, but there she was, hanging upside down but not hurt! Our daughter had just come from the back seat to the front and was sitting between us. We were singing "The Lord's Prayer". The instant we began to lose control of the car, we were singing "Thy will be done".

We crawled out of the car on the driver's side and stood in the rain. Soon a car came along, stopped, and the driver said to me, "Albeit, the driver never survived that wreck." I told him that the three of us just crawled out of there with only a few cuts and bruises. God was watching over us, but my beautiful 1967 Pontiac was wrecked.

CHAPTER 14

Back to Pennsylvania

I purchased a twenty-one-acre piece of woodland from my foster mother near Belleville as an investment. I thought if I would ever move back to Pennsylvania, I would be able to use this ground for a cabin. Sammie and I had cut trees there when I was a teenager and I had lots of memories of hunting small game in those woods. So on Memorial Day of 1971, just two weeks before we planned to move, we came back to Belleville and built a little 16x24 cabin on this piece of woods so that we could live there until we built or bought a home.

On June 17, we said goodbye to our friends at the oil company. I loaded a large U-Haul truck and my van with all of our belongings, and we moved back to Belleville. We moved into Katie's brother's basement first and stored some of our things. I remember that Urie's wife, Rachel, went to school in Allensville at the same time that I did and she sat right across the aisle from me. Rachel was fourteen and I was fifteen. She was cute too. That was in 1950 and now it was 1971. She was married to Katie's brother and we were temporarily living in their basement. It goes to say you just never know what you are going to do in your life.

After we moved into the cabin and began to make it livable, I told my wife that we could build two more large rooms against the end and just live there. Mother had given permission to the neighbor years before to lay a water line across her land and she told the neighbor to give her a free everlasting water tap at a place she requested. This was smart thinking on her part as now I owned the land and I had that water tap with the best mountain water you could ever ask for. So, we just dug down to the tap and hooked on. What a blessing! We soon saw that we had wonderful neighbors all around us and they helped us get started. I decided to make this cabin idea into a full sized house.

As the summer of 1971 went by, I taught our fourteen year old daughter, Nancy, to be a carpenter as we worked long days at our future home and by the early part of August we moved into our house. True, it was not all completed but it was good enough to live in. We invited some of our friends and relatives to help us.

Since I did not have a job yet, we decided to take

a trip to the west coast and see the Pacific Ocean. So, we loaded the Ford window van with some cooking utensils and camping equipment. A friend of Nancy's, Judy Zook, traveled with us to Sweet Home, Oregon, where she had relatives. We were on the road for almost a month as we went north through Canada and through the northwestern states into Washington and Oregon. We dropped Judy off at her relatives and visited with them for several days.

Mr. and Mrs. Sam Zook had three teenage daughters at home and they were glad to see Judy. He had a big logging truck and he took me up into the mountains where they harvest those big trees. I was very much impressed with the giant trees. The back of the truck extended so they could load seventy to one hundred foot long trees on the trailer-type truck. The back of the trailer trailed in the tracks of the front wheels, making it possible for the truck to go around sharp turns. We took a tour through the sawmill that processed these huge trees and we watched them make plywood and posts. Nothing was wasted. After we left Oregon and Judy safe with her relatives, the three of us went southeast to Nevada, Utah, Colorado, and many other states.

Soon after we returned to Belleville, I began working for my neighbor Caleb Peachey who was in the excavating business. We did a lot of work in the few years that I spent working with him. I remember he had a sign on the side of his truck that said, "We Move the Earth" and we did!

I started my own construction business in the summer of 1978 and I purchased my first backhoe in 1981. When I had big jobs, I would hire men that owned their own equipment to do the digging for me. One very special person that I have learned to appreciate is Sam Hostetler, who owns Sam's Backhoe Service. Sam and his wife, with their four boys, have been a great blessing to me. I treat him just like a son. We did a lot of big jobs together and we still get together to hunt and fish.

The majority of the time I would work by myself because most of my water and sewer line work was connecting houses to central sewage and water systems. I had my daughter helping me during the summer of 1981 laying sewer pipes in the town of Milroy. She got to know her dad a lot more than she ever did. I have said that a lot of my work is under the ground and will be there when Jesus comes back to take us up to heaven.

My new Ford backhoe, purchased in 1981.

CHAPTER 15

Hard Times for My Foster Parents

My mother and father experienced a decisive, busy year in 1971. My younger sister, Janie, called me just before she was to go to Florida with our parents. "I am so tired of Mother bossing me around that I have decided to run away and not go to Florida with them," she told me. "I want you to pick me up at the neighbor's lane and take me somewhere out of the area."

I hated to get involved with this situation but I did meet her early the next morning around five o'clock. We crossed the Seven Mountains to a town called Spring Mills, where she stayed with some of Mother's friends. The next morning when Mother and Father got ready to go south, Janie was nowhere to be found! I went to work right after I dropped her off and acted like nothing ever happened. However, inside I was hurting badly because I knew that Mother would find out that I helped Janie leave the farm and she would be very upset with me. I said to myself, "What does a person do when he gets between a rock and a hard place!" That is the way it was.

Janie found a job near her temporary home and went to work at a factory in Spring Mills. While she was working there, she met a man named David Immel, who worked at the same place. In the spring of 1972, she married him at Rebersburg. Soon after that, they moved to Sarasota, Florida, where they stayed for quite awhile. Later they moved back to Big Valley and he worked for Metz Hatchery for a time. They were blessed with five boys and one girl, so they had lots of challenges! Mother's disappointment with Janie running away gradually healed over time. Mother gave Janie and her family an acre of woodland on which to build a house.

The Metz Hatchery apartment where they presently lived was too small for five children, so David and Jane built a very small house on that property. They really had a struggle to survive. Sammie and I soon saw that they needed a lot more space, so we built a two-story addition for decent bedrooms. We also purchased a station wagon for them. They wanted to get telephone service but the neighbors did not like the Peter Tumbledown look so they would not give a right of way for phone service. Jane and her family lived there for several years, before moving to the Center County area.

In November of 1972, my foster father, Monroe Mohler, passed away at the age of 92. His mind was very good until a month or so before his death. He was buried beside his first wife in the Weaverland Mennonite Cemetery near Terry Hill, Pa. Thus ended a wonderful time I had for twenty-five years learning things from him.

In 1979, Mother was having so much pain with her arthritis that she tried almost anything for comfort. She heard of a place out in Montana where you could go down in this uranium mine for a while and this would supposedly help your joints. Mother asked me if I would drive her and Sammie out to Montana and they would stay there for two weeks to try this new treatment. In the meantime, I would fly home. Then she would drive back home herself. Well, on the way out, she began to complain to me how the money goes so fast for everything you buy. I told her that she might as well spend it for what she wants now, because it would look funny to be taken to the cemetery in a hearse towing a U-haul trailer with all your belongings in it.

At first she giggled about that, then she got upset and said, "Yes, you just can hardly wait until I die so you can get my money." I said it only for a joke but it rubbed her the wrong way.

After Dad died, Lizzie became frustrated with Mother's attitude. One day when they were in the basement working, Mother got angry with Lizzie and threw a hatchet at her. Lizzie had lived with Mother for over fifty years. The next day Sammie and Mother went to Lewistown and while they were there, Lizzie called my wife. She said that she was leaving Mother's place and moving to her friend's house on Pleasant Avenue in Belleville. Rudy and Mattie Renno came up to my Mother's house to get Lizzie. She left a note on the table for Mother. When Mother and Sammie came back from town, there was this note on the table that said Lizzie did not want to live with Katie Mae, as she often was called, any more. Mother became angry because she realized that her world was falling apart.

She went down to Belleville and found where Lizzie was staying. She said to her, "Now I want you to come back home where you belong!"

However, Mattie was standing in front of Lizzie and she said, "She is not coming back with you so just turn around and go back home!"

Mother saw that she could not win this case and she said to Sammie, "Are you also going to run off too?"

Sammie said, "No, I will stay with you."

During the winter of 1977, while Mother was in Florida she suffered a stroke and was not able to drive her car. I took some time off and got on a plane going south to stay with her. After a few days, I drove her and the car back to Belleville. This was very hard on me because I could not talk with her. Mother's stroke affected her speech and all the fun times were lost because we could not communicate with each other. I would ask her questions just to see how bad her stroke had affected her memory, and she would say four words "I just cannot say".

Mother and Sammie were the only ones on the farm now, because Janie and Lizzie left the farm in frustration. The two of them could not keep up with things. In the spring of 1978, as Mother was improving, she decided to sell all the farm animals and just survive with Sammie there to help her. They rented the fields out to the neighbors and went to Florida in the wintertime.

In the winter of 1981, on January 26, Mother passed away at her home in Sarasota. She developed a bad cough after the evening meal, and the doctor said she died from heart failure. This ended an era of living with my mother and spending days on the farm. When she died, she willed the farm to one of her nephews. As I write this book, in 2004, her nephew still owns the farm; however, it has fallen into some disrepair. It is typical of so many large farms of today. The farm was such a wonderful part of my heritage and it saddens me to see it in such a state.

Sammie told me a lot of things about Mother after she died and it would take many pages for me to tell all about it. I was told that she would go to a person's home and pow-wow. I think this was done to help cure their ills. (For my non-Amish readers, the practice of pow-wow is still done in some communities where the folks have more confidence in their own members than in modern doctors.) I never knew that Mother practiced this.

Sammie was always such a meek and mild man and I felt so sorry for him. He told me that a better day was coming. Of course, he meant Heaven! However, he did not know that something else wonderful was going to happen sooner than he expected.

Sammie went back to Florida soon after Mother's death. However, before he left, he went to see Lizzie. He told her that he would like to have her come and live with him. Almost like a brother and sister, they had lived together on the farm for more than fifty years and they understood each other. Mother was gone and so were the problems that they had with her. He needed a cook and house keeper, so Lizzie went to Florida to live in the same home where they had lived before when Mother was living. On March 4, 1982, we received a phone call from Florida saying Sammie and Lizzie had just gotten married! I said, "Where did you ever hear such a crazy thing like that?"

Sammie and Lizzie, taken in Sarasota, Florida, soon after their wedding day, March 4, 1982.

Needless to say, we were shocked, but happy! I asked Mother years before, why Sammie and Lizzie never got married, and she about threw a fit, saying I was crazy to say such a thing! Well, now Mother had been dead for a while and they were married. I believe if she had known, she would have turned over in her grave! Katie and I soon left for Florida to see the happy couple. Sammie was 73, Lizzie was

70, and they had never been married before. So you see what I meant when I said to Sammie, "Is this the time now when you said there's a better day coming?" We had a hearty laugh about that! In addition, we hugged each other and rejoiced because now they could share their lives in a different perspective.

My wife and I went to the local shopping center; bought them a nice set of silverware, and shared the excitement of these newlyweds. Sammie and Lizzie lived happily together. In 1983, they sold their house that they were married in and bought a smaller house in Pinecraft, near Sarasota, Florida.

My wife and I went to Florida each winter for a short time with our boat and spent two weeks of fun, fishing and visiting with Sammie and Lizzie. In 1986, they sold their house and purchased a cottage at

Katie and George in 1982.

Belleville. We loaded the boat and our van with most of their belongings and two other friends with station wagons helped them move into their cottage in the Valley View Retirement Village. Sammie and Lizzie are now both deceased. It is hard to see your dear friends age. I told Sammie one day that he should stop driving his car because he could not remember how to get back to the village.

He said, "Do you want to take my car away from me?"

I said, "I'm so sorry but it is in your best interest." It made me cry for a while.

Sammie developed a fast growing leukemia that took his life. Lizzie lived several more years at the nursing home. My wife and I stayed with them to the end. However, as long as I am of sound mind, I will have many memories of those precious years.

CHAPTER 16

Our Family Grows

When we moved back to Pennsylvania, from Ohio, our daughter, Nancy, attended Kishacoquillas High School. She was a very good student, graduating top in her class in commercial studies, which included bookkeeping, typing, and shorthand. After graduation, she began working as a typesetter for the local weekly newspapers, *The Valley Observer* and *This Week In Mifflin County* now simply called *The County Observer*.

She went through her share of teenage struggles as she learned to develop her independence. She bought her first car, a small Mercury Capri. However, that following winter, during a terrible snowstorm with blizzard conditions, she crested the Belleville hill and ran into the back of another car. The car was demolished and she needed quite a few stitches in her chin. However, we were glad that it was not worse. Her next car was a yellow and black Ford Maverick. The reason that I tell you this is it eventually led to her meeting a very special person in her life.

Nancy would talk about this boy or that boy she had met, but my wife would say to her different times that they were related to us. My wife's maiden name was Yoder and there are many people with the last name Yoder in our area. So Nancy decided she was going to Lewistown to look for a husband. Believe me, my wife, and I did a great deal of praying. Nancy said, "I know I can't get into too much trouble because Mom is home praying for me."

We believe in the power of prayer, because in the spring of 1977 we were introduced to our future son-in-law, James Williams. They met in the parking lot behind the Bon Ton Department store and he had a red and black Ford Maverick. I think the cars had something to do with their first conversation.

They were married the following year on June 24, 1978, at the Allensville Presbyterian Church. It was a beautiful day and since we only have the one daughter, I decided that we were going to do it right. We invited over three hundred people to the wedding and the reception, which was held at the Belleville Community Hall. We had a full course ham dinner for the noon meal. It was a wonderful day, one I shall never forget.

Nancy wanted me to sing *The Lord's Prayer* at the wedding and I was honored that she asked, but when

Our daughter, Nancy, and her husband, Jim Williams, on their wedding day, June 24, 1978.

the time came for me to sing, I turned to my wife and said, "I don't know if I can do this." She said, "Yes, you can!" And I did, but I think it was harder than walking Nancy down the isle.

Jim has been a wonderful addition to our family. He likes to hunt and fish, so we immediately had many things in common. He is a hard working man and not afraid to step right in to help with projects, and that means a great deal to me. He works at a local plastic manufacturing plant as a maintenance machinist. He has helped me out on numerous occasions, building me things for different jobs.

In the fall of 1982, Nancy and Jim gave us some wonderful news. We were going to be grandparents. At first I was not too sure I liked the idea of being a grandpa, but when our granddaughter, Lenette, arrived in April, it was love at first sight. It is amazing to me what a baby will do to a person who feels he is not old enough to be a grandpa! Our second granddaughter, Diana, arrived almost four years later in February of 1987.

I am holding my first granddaughter,
Lenette Marie Williams.

When Lenette started school, I made a deal with her. I told her I would give her a dollar for every "A" she got on her report card. In addition, as she went from grade to grade, I would pay her a dollar for the year grade. Therefore, when she went into second grade it was two dollars for every A, and so on. By her senior year, it was costing me $96 every time she brought home her report card. In addition, of course, Diana has received the same treatment. After all, you cannot do for one without the other. As far as I can remember, Lenette always got A's and Diana, too.

I told a number of people that it may have cost me thousands of dollars, but it was the best incentive program that the girls will have for getting good grades. In addition, it has worked. They are both excellent students and believe me; they let me know when it is report card time! We watched Lenette give a speech in June of 2000, as she graduated third in her class. Now she is attending college. No, I am not paying for her grades in college, but she is still getting all "A's". Diana is a student in high school and is following in her sister's footsteps as far as the "A's" go.

My wife and I are very proud of our girls. They are growing into wonderful young women. Both girls are very gifted. Lenette is an accounting major and

Our daughter and family. Left to right: Jim, Nancy, Diana, and Lenette Williams, March 2005.

is minoring in music at Elizabethtown College. She is also a talented musician who loves to sing, play the piano, flute, and bassoon. Diana is active in 4-H, and has won several grand champion awards at the county fair in cake decorating, folk art, pottery, sewing, woodworking, and quilting. She is also a musician, playing the saxophone in the marching band. Her senior year, she served as yearbook editor. She plans to pursue a career in advertising and graphic design.

Nancy and her family are also very involved in their church. It is a joy to see that your child and your grandchildren follow the way of faith. The most important lesson we can teach our children is a love for God and a relationship with Jesus Christ. It is never too early to begin teaching your children responsibility, love for other people, "The Ten Commandments", and the verse in the Bible that say's "Do unto others as you would have them do unto you".

I realize that I myself did not always do as I was told to do, but as I grow older I know that the following things are very important: integrity, honesty, to hold no grudges, and do not go to bed angry! I worked very hard in my life and I could work circles around many young people. My foster mother used to say, "Management is half of the work."

CHAPTER 17

Children Together Again

In 1940 when my real mother left my brother, sister, and me at the Millersville Children Home, I thought she was gone forever from our lives. I want the readers to know that my foster mother knew all along where my brother and sister lived but she felt that the less we saw of each other the better off we would be. I remember a situation when I was thirteen. I was lying in my bed crying for my real mother. My foster mother came to the bedroom door and said, "Be quiet! Your parents didn't love you then and they wouldn't want you now, so forget about them."

In the summer of 1954, Monroe and Katie took me to visit some of his sons who lived in Ephrata,

Pennsylvania. On Sunday, we went to Gehmans Mennonite Church for the Sunday morning services. I was sitting beside my stepbrother Bill, watching the people coming in to the church when several teenage girls were walking along the windows. They were dressed in the traditional Mennonite clothes, which included little white caps on their heads. Bill leaned over to me and said, "Did you know that one girl is your sister Nancy?" It was just like a bombshell to me. I was 19 years old and she was 16! My heart almost exploded and I could not take my eyes off of her. I had not seen her since she was a little baby at the orphanage. After church, we went to the pastor's house for a meal and I discovered they had raised a few children, including my baby sister.

Nancy did not remember anything about her mother, brother, or me, although her foster parents did tell her that she had a brother and sister. We did a lot of talking about our growing up years. I told her that I knew that our mother's name was Esther and our brother's name was Bobby. I told her that Bob's foster parents, whose name was Shank, had brought him to the farm to visit when I was fourteen, but that was the end of any more contacts. I was so glad to realize that I now had my sister in my life! However, after that day, my foster parents and I went back to the farm and any more contact with my siblings was discouraged. It seemed so cruel to be apart and not see each other during our growing up years.

On my wedding day, September 15, 1956, my foster mother had arranged to have my brother and sister come and be in the wedding party! However, after the wedding, we went to our separate homes and did not see each other again for more than ten years.

In 1967, while my wife and I and our 10-year-old daughter lived in Ohio, one day out of the blue, a letter came from my sister, Nancy. She just came home from the hospital with her fourth child! Gee, I did not even know that she was married! We wasted no time driving from Massillon, Ohio, to Reading, Pennsylvania. Nancy and her husband, Jerry Paris, had four children: two girls, April and Tina, and two boys, Jerry Jr. and John Paul. We had a lot of catching up to do about things that happened since my wedding eleven years before.

While we were there, I said to my sister, "I wonder where our brother is? I have not seen him since my wedding day. If we only knew where he might live, we could maybe solve this mystery."

My sister said she thought he may have gone into the service and that a farmer near Strasburg raised him, but she did not know any more than that. We decided he could be married or far away. One place to check was the Lancaster, Pennsylvania, phone directory, so I called the operator Saturday evening and asked her if she had a listing for a Robert Kloepfer in the Lancaster area. Soon she said, "No, but there is one in the Strasburg directory."

I got that number and tried to dial, but no one was at home. I told my sister I would try Sunday morning around 8:30 a.m. I dialed again and a woman with a pleasant voice said, "Hello, Kloepfers."

My heart was pounding as I wondered if this was my brother's place! I tried to be casual and said, "Sure is a lovely day and what are your plans?"

She said, "We are ready to go to church and after

that it is our annual family reunion."

Luckily, she did not ask who I was because I wanted to hear Bob's voice, so I said, "Is Bob available?"

She said, "One moment, please."

Then Bob came on the phone and said, "Hello."

I said, "It sounds like you have a busy day."

"Yes," he said.

Then I said, "Didn't you tell me that you had a sister named Nancy?"

"Yes," he said, "but I have not seen her in many years and I do not know where she lives."

I said, "Don't you have a brother named George?"

By this time, he was wondering who he was talking to, and said, "Who is this?"

Well, I was so nervous I said in a shaking voice, "This is your brother George."

"What! Where are you?"

I said, "I am at our sister's home in Galen Hall, a trailer park just west of Reading, Pennsylvania, and we would love to see you!"

He said they would try to come up around 4:00 pm.

I said, "If we only knew what happened to our parents it would make the mystery so much easier to solve. Nancy said she knows nothing about them."

About 1:30 that Sunday afternoon, Bob and his wife drove into the park in his red convertible! His wife said that after that phone call in the morning his mind seemed to be in another world and he just couldn't wait to get to his sister's house! We took some pictures of all of us so we would have those precious memories. That was the beginning of a permanent relationship between brothers and sister!

So the mystery was partly solved. I said to my

My siblings, Bob, Nancy, and I, taken in 1967, reunited again.

brother, "If we could only find our parents, we would be complete!"

He said, "Apparently they did not want us then and they would likely be a burden to us later if we did find them."

Well, I said, "If I could only look across a backyard fence and look at them, even if they would not want to speak to me, I would be satisfied." I was wrong!

My brother Bob and I had a slightly different view on finding our biological parents. He did not remember them at all, but I remembered my mother and wanted desperately to find out what had happened to her. A strict Mennonite family raised Bob on a farm, but he chose not to become a farmer. He met a Christian girl in the early 1960s named Donna and they were married. They had two children, Kristine and Bobby Jr. After our reunion in 1967, we kept in touch and spent holidays visiting back and forth.

Donna developed breast cancer in the early 1980s. Ten years later, it took her life. Her death was very hard on all of us, as we had become quite close. Before she died, she asked me to sing a song at her funeral. I did, but it was not easy for me. The children missed her as a loving mother. They are grown now, married, with families of their own. Kristine lives in Lampeter with her husband, Troy Becker, and their children, Georgia and Evan. Bobby is married to Dawn and they have three sons. My brother, Bob, is remarried to a pleasant woman named Margaret, and they live in Willow Street, Pennsylvania.

George, Nancy, and Bob. Taken at Nancy's home at Osceola, PA, in 2002.

CHAPTER 18

A Day to Remember

In the summer of 1973, I was working on a job in Harrisburg installing water and sewer lines for a large development called Camelot Village. I was the job supervisor for Caleb J. Peachey Excavating. The job phone rang around 10:30 in the morning and I answered it. My wife was on the other end, saying she had just received a call from my sister Nancy, who had visited my real mother.

I said, "You mean my real mother, Esther?"

"Yes," she said, "and she lives in Lebanon, Pennsylvania, with her husband, Jack Dealy. She would love to see you." So, a week or so after I got over my shock, I traveled with my wife and daughter from Belleville to Lebanon.

It was a beautiful day in August and people were sitting out on the sidewalk. As we drove in front of this apartment, my wife said to me, "That lady on the lawn chair has to be your mother!" I said I would drive down two car lengths and then I would go back and ask her if she might know where a Mrs. Dealy lives. I just wanted to play it cool!

I parked the car and asked my daughter Nancy to walk with me, and then we began to walk toward her. I was almost ready to ask the question when she jumped up out of her chair. She grabbed me and just held on! Finally, she let go and looked in my eyes. With a tense expression, she asked me, "You won't hold it against me that I put you in an orphanage will you?"

I said, "No, Mother, that is history. Sure, I have a lot of questions, but I won't hold it against you."

Then she started to cry, and I cried too. I was so glad to have her in my life. We hugged for a while and cried, as I am crying now as I write this story. I get many flashbacks and I think, if only we could change the past. We all went inside their house and she introduced us to her husband. He had been in the military years before. They had met in Newport News, Va., and now they were together for a long time.

The following story is like a fairy tale, but it is not. Mother shared this information with me in detail. She said soon after her daughter was taken from the orphanage, she found out that Rev. and Mrs. Paul Martin adopted her. Mother was like Mary in the Bible. She pondered these things in her heart. Should she go and look for her or not? However, she decided that she should not go. Mother shared her life and about her children with her neighbors over the years.

Many years later, there was a picture of two women coming out of a new department store called Two Guys on the front page of the Reading newspaper. The upstairs neighbor called down the steps and said to mother, "There is a picture of two women on the front page of today's paper and the one lady looks just like you! Her name is Nancy Louise Martin!"

Mother said, "Throw that paper down the steps when you are done with it; I want to see it." Mother cut the article out of the paper and put it in her treasure chest. She was sure it was her own daughter, Nancy Louise!

Several years later, the upstairs neighbor said to her one day, "I see in the paper where a Nancy Louise Martin is engaged to a Jerry Paris, with their address listed here. Didn't you say that your daughter is named Nancy Louise Martin?"

"Yes," mother said. "May I have the paper when you are done with it?" Mother cut that part out and put it in her treasure chest too. Now she had her daughter's married name and address. However, she still lacked the courage to go and visit.

Finally, in 1973 Jack and Mother drove to Reading, Pennsylvania, on a Sunday afternoon. Mother was anxious to see if she could find the address of Jerry Paris that was listed on the paper clipping she had saved from years before. They did find the street and Mother went up to the door and knocked. A woman came to the door, so Mother introduced herself and said she was looking for a Nancy Paris. The woman she spoke to at the door was Nancy's mother-in-law, who took one look at Mother and realized who she was. She told her that Nancy and her family were camping, but she would give them the message. She took Mother's address and phone number.

Nancy was married for many years and had four children by this time. Mrs. Paris called Nancy Sunday evening after they got home from their camping trip. She told her that a woman had been there in the afternoon and she had to be Nancy's mother, because she looked just like her. She gave Nancy her address and phone number and said that the woman had wanted to talk to her. In the mean time, Mother and Jack went back to Lebanon wondering if Nancy would call them the next week.

Monday morning the phone rang and it was Nancy calling Mother, saying that she wanted to come to Lebanon and visit her, which she did. They had a wonderful reunion. Nancy had always wanted to find her real mother and was thrilled to finally be reunited with her. Nancy showed Mother some pictures of us that were taken when we had visited Nancy back in 1967 in the trailer park six years before! That is how Mother recognized me when I walked up to her on that special day in front of her house in Lebanon! When Nancy went back to her home, she called my wife, who in turn called me on the job phone in Harrisburg that glorious Monday morning.

Several years later, Mother's husband, Jack, fell in the bathtub. Later he died of complications, so Mother was a widow again. The next year she went to live with my sister Nancy, and was there until our daughter married in 1978 when she moved to our home at Belleville. Now we could catch up with some of our life that was missed!

I introduced my biological mother to my foster mother and took them both out to dinner on Mothers' Day a year or so before my foster mother passed away. It is not very often that a man takes two mothers out to dinner at one time!

While my mother lived with us, she became a special member of our family. We took her along to church and introduced her to all of our friends. She grew up attending the Church of the Brethren near Palmyra, but had not really attended church regularly. Mother told me a lot of wild stories and funny jokes. She had a wonderful sense of humor. She also told me what her life was like with my real dad. My father was George William Kloepfer. He was born on January

My mother's family. Front row, left to right: Pharas, Alice (Groff) Reider, Almeda, Edward Reider, and Esther. Back row, left to right: Shirley, Harrison, Gertrude, Roy, and Ada.

7, 1909. My parents were married on February 6, 1934, in Elton, Maryland. My mother, who was born on June 1, 1915, grew up in Palmyra, Pennsylvania, and attended the Church of the Brethren there. This was during the Great Depression. She had seven brothers and sisters: Gertrude, Roy, Ada, Harrison, Shirley, Phares, and Almeda (who is the only one still living).

Her parents were not too thrilled when she ran off and got married to my dad. However, my parents were young and in love. They operated a dog kennel in Elizabeth, New Jersey, after they were married. I was born January 26, 1935, in the Kimball Hospital in Lakewood, New Jersey. They were very excited for their firstborn son. On February 6, 1937, my brother, Robert Fred, was born. Then another year later on June 3, 1938, a daughter, Nancy Louise, was born. Their business eventually failed and jobs became hard to find.

My parents, George and Esther Kloepfer, in New Jersey.

Dad was always trying to find better jobs and they were not always better. He would leave Mother for weeks at a time without a word. When he would come home, she would always take him back. Soon after, she would find herself pregnant again. At one point, Dad worked as a laborer, helping to build the Pentagon in Washington, DC. Once he found a job in Atlantic City, for himself and one for Mother. He wanted her to be a waitress and tend bar in this fancy place. He told her to come to be with him, and that he had a place for them to live close by. Mother said, "Do you want me to come with three little children and tend bar? Forget it and I am forgetting you."

That is why Mother took my brother, sister, and me to Palmyra, Pennsylvania, where we moved in with her brother Roy, my uncle, for a while. As time passed, my Uncle Roy said to Mother, "Why don't you put the children in an orphanage for awhile until you get some money and a place of your own? The children are getting on my nerves." Therefore, Mother had to put us in the orphanage until she could get on her feet.

Once she had a place of her own, she came to the orphanage to take us home with her. Unfortunately, my brother was already placed in someone's home, so the superintendent said she should come back later. When she did come back, I was at someone's house and my brother was back in the orphanage. So she said she would try again another time. Mother tried to get us later, when we were all back in the home. She told the superintendent that she had a place and could afford to keep us now. However, the superintendent said, "It is the policy of the home that if the parents want the children back, which they seldom do, they must reimburse the home for the expenses incurred while they are here."

So my mother asked, "How much would that be?"

He said, "Three hundred dollars!"

Mother said, "Three hundred dollars! I could never come up with that much money."

The superintendent said, "Sorry, but that is our policy." Mother left the home crying bitterly, hating the orphanage, and never coming back. That is how she lost her children. It was not her desire, but times were hard back then, with no governmental programs for assistance. She told me that she cried for a year after she lost her children. Finally, her brother said that she had to get on with her life. Later, she got a job working in a shoe factory for many years.

Mother answered many questions for me about our early life together and about my father. She said he always had "itchy feet" and could not stay in one place very long. Maybe that is why I love to travel so much.

Mother gave me my father's death certificate, which she had received in 1956. It said he died in California of heart disease. Mother was upset when she got that death certificate because it stated that he was never married. She said, "How could he lie like that?"

My brother Bob was not quite as anxious to be reunited with Mother as Nancy and I were. I think he was afraid that she had come back into our lives for an ulterior motive. However, it bothered me that Bob did not want to see Mother. Therefore, I took matters into my own hands.

Some Amish friends ask me to take them to Lancaster to visit their family at Christmas time. I took my wife, daughter, future son-in-law, and my mother Esther along for the day. She was visiting us over the holidays.

While we were in Lancaster, I said to Mother, "Let's go over to Bob's house and see what they are doing." Mother knew that Bob did not really want to see her, so she was nervous. Up until this time, Bob had not wanted to see Mother because he did not remember any thing of her. A number of years had passed since my sister and I had found Mother. I really wanted to see all of the family together again.

When we first arrived at Bob's home, my daughter, Nancy, and her fiancé went to the door. As it had been a long time since Bob had seen my daughter, he did not recognize her at first. Then I went to the door and surprised Bob.

"I have Mother in the car and she would like to meet you," I said. "But if you do not want to see her, she will understand and will wait in the car until we are done visiting."

Bob said, "Oh, what the heck, bring her in."

I went out to the car and said to Mother, "He said you could come in." Now my heart was pounding because I had put Bob in a difficult position. I wondered if he would accept Mother or not.

We went in and sat down in their living room and Bob's lovely wife, Donna, served us cookies and drinks. It was a very tense time. Bob pretended that Mother was not there. I thought, "Dear brother, how can you be so cruel."

Finally, it was time to go, so I thought I would give

Bob one more chance. I waited until everyone was out the door except Mother, who was behind me. As Bob was holding the door, I heard this little swish. I looked around and saw Bob take Mother into his arms! I was so happy and so was Mother. When we got into the car, she began to shed happy tears and said, "I have not cried since I lost you children, but now I have my children back again." Needless to say, we all cried for quite a while with Mother.

George, Nancy, Bob, and our mother, Esther.

Mother had a bad habit that I tried to break her of and that was smoking. It used to be said that you cannot teach an old dog new tricks and I guess that is the way it was with Mother. She had smoked for many years and even spent time in a tuberculosis sanitarium where they told her, "No more smoking!" However, she had a stubborn streak.

She lived with us for several years. Her bad habit finally started to affect my wife's throat and breathing. I said to Mother, "Please think about quitting smoking. It would be good for us all." However, she said she enjoyed smoking and would move out and get a place of her own before she would quit.

Mother had one sister living near Lebanon, Pennsylvania, and between the two of them, they found an apartment in a state owned housing complex. We helped Mother move into that place, and she really enjoyed living there. We visited her many times until her death on May 15, 2000. She would have been 85 on her next birthday.

Mother wanted to be cremated and I had the graveside services. My friend, Tim Peachey, gave me

Visiting Mother at her apartment in Lebanon, Pa., June 1997.
Left to right: daughter Nancy, Mother, granddaughters
Lenette and Diana, and George.

a book to use about funeral services. I shared with the group that Mother loved us children and wanted us to all be together as a family, but she was the victim of hard times. We buried her in the Colebrook Church Cemetery on a sunny afternoon with a good number of relatives and friends in attendance. My brother, sister, and I purchased a nice tombstone and I placed it at her gravesite beside my Uncle Roy.

So ends an era of my life with my real mother, but I am thankful that I have many memories!

CHAPTER 19

The Hunter

During my teenage years, I developed a desire to hunt. There were lots of rabbits and pheasants in the fields and I decided to make a bow and arrow! I knew that the dogwood tree had lots of strength and would bend but not break. So I got a nice center of a tree and I sawed a bow out of it on our table saw in the wood shop. Then I went out to the orchard and found some nice straight apple tree sprouts. I trimmed all the burrs off the arrows, and fastened nails for the points and glued some goose feathers on them for fletching. I practiced on a straw bale. I did not shoot any animals, but I tried.

I developed more accuracy throwing small stones.

In hunting season, I could hit a rabbit when it was sitting in its nest under a clump of grass in the pasture field. I got a few rabbits that way. As I was walking along the cow path, this redwing blackbird would always fly up and make a big fuss as I passed its hiding place. I decided I had enough of that, so I took a small round stone and threw it right at the bird. The bird could not dodge the stone. As I think back, it seems kind of nasty but it is history now. I felt like King David in the Bible. A little stone can do wonders if thrown at the right place!

Something else I used to do in hunting season that seemed impossible was catching wild rabbits with my bare hands! I would watch where rabbits would sit under a thick clump of grass, and then I would get down on my belly, crawl slowly to the cluster of grass, and grab the rabbit before it knew what happened. Some times, I would let it go and other times we would have rabbit for supper.

When I was sixteen, I asked my mother if I could have her 22 rifle to go hunting. She said I could, although I must finish the chores first. I soon had some rabbits, squirrels, and a pheasant, too. I used to enjoy going into the hog pen an hour after dark with the 22 rifle loaded with fine shot to shoot the rats that came from every where to eat the hog feed. They usually stayed in the corncrib during the daytime, but at night, it was full of rats. Many a rat died of lead poisoning those nights. But one night, a rat ran straight towards me and tried to crawl up my pant leg. That scared me about half to death, so the rats had a break from me for a while until I got over that scare!

When I was seventeen, I asked Mother again if I could have her gun when hunting season came around, but this time she said, "No, you spent too much time last fall and I want you to forget about hunting this year." Well, that was a terrible pill to swallow. Soon Mother and Father went to Florida and I thought to myself, I really do not need her gun. I will make a gun myself. I went to the shop and found a long drill just the size of a 22 bullet and a piece of one-inch steel bar about ten inches long. I drilled a hole right down the center of it. I took another short piece of steel the same size as the long piece and I drilled a small hole just a little offset from the other piece so a nail put in that hole would just be right to hit the primer. I drilled a hole on the top at each end of the long piece. I fastened a nail into those holes and used them for sights. Then I set this into a piece of pine two by four that I hollowed out as a stock. I also shaped a short piece of steel and a spring for a trigger assembly and that just worked fine! Now I thought, I am ready for hunting season. So, when the time came, I went out and had a lot of fun showing my homemade 22 to my friends and I shot a few rabbits and one ring-necked pheasant too. Sammie did not know what to think of my gun, but Lizzie thought it was just great!

While Mother was in Florida, she would usually call home every two weeks to hear what was happening on the farm. Sammie would give a report on which cows would freshen and what was done in the fields. She asked especially what I was doing. Sammie told her I had just finished cleaning the stables and was doing some hunting too. Mother said, "Hunting! I told you not to give him my gun this year!" Sammie told her I made a 22.

A day or so later as we were working in the barn, two men came driving into the barnyard. Sammie went out to talk to them and I recognized the one man as the game warden that lived in Belleville. I tried to listen to the conversation. Soon Sammie called, telling me the men wanted to talk to me. They said politely, "Sammie tells us that you are a good hunter and you made a gun." I was delighted to show them my gun and how it worked. One of the men said, "I am very sorry, but we have to take this gun with us. It is illegal to make your own gun without a license from the government."

I was heartbroken about this whole affair although I knew that Mother did not want me to hunt. So that is the way it was and there was no more hunting that year. I found out later that Mother had called the warden and told them about my gun. I developed a negative feeling towards Mother for a long time after that!

One day before the 1953, hunting season began; Lizzie called me into the house. Mother had already left for Florida, so there was peace around the farm. Lizzie said, "I have something to give you." She handed me a long box and as I opened the box, I got very excited. Lizzie and Sammie had driven to Lewistown and Lizzie bought me a brand new Marlin 22 bolt action from Montgomery Ward. Lizzie said, "I pitied you so much last year when those men came and took your gun away, so I wanted to do this for you." I was eighteen and this rifle was mine. She said she paid $18.50 for it.

This was the beginning of a long period of making

new friends and going hunting. I bought an old 7.07 Japanese rifle, converted to 30.06, through the mail and then I could go deer hunting. I went with a group of hunters led by three men, David T. Yoder, Mark Yoder, and John Kurtz. We were called the Peachey gang, sometimes called the meat hounds, because we got lots of deer! Those were the days when you could take up to fifty men and comb the mountain. Now you are only allowed up to twenty-five fellows. We went all over central Pennsylvania for many years. I had loads of fun but tired legs. (Maybe that is why my hips are starting to wear out now. I am just sixty-nine, but I sometimes wonder how my legs have taken a beating all these years and have held up for so long.) We did shoot a lot of deer and a few bears, although I never shot a bear. I remember many times that I crawled under the laurel bushes on my hands and knees through the snow trying to spook out those deer and bears!

In 1958, I traded in the 7.07 Japanese rifle for a new Remington model 722, 244 caliber rifle with a ten-power scope. Since that time, I have shot hundreds of groundhogs, crows and many deer. A hunting experience I recall happened when we lived in the town of White Hall in 1960. It was the last day of deer season and eight inches of new snow fell the night before. I decided to walk across the fields to the mountain and hunt a section of woods that I was familiar with. As I walked, I prayed to God to please help me to see a buck to shoot, because we needed the meat. It turned out to be a little tiresome walking through the snow as it was deeper in the woods. As I walked slowly down this narrow strip of trees and brush, I noticed three does get up from their beds and slowly walk away. I stopped for a while and cased that area, then slowly made my way to where the does had been laying.

Suddenly I saw a nice buck with spikes maybe six or seven inches long laying there, chewing his cud, unaware of my presence. I slowly raised my rifle and took careful aim. I thought of my request to God and how He showed me this buck. I fully expected to see a dead deer after I shot, but to my surprise the buck jumped up, ran off and jumped over the nearby fence. I was so shocked I never thought of shooting again as it ran out of sight.

When I realized that I missed this buck I just cried for a while because I was very distraught. Then I thanked God for showing me the deer, and realized it was my responsibility to shoot it.

About three months later, I was in the same area checking Mother's fence line as we planned to put cattle in the field to spring pasture. I walked over to the now historic spot to relive the sad memory, when I noticed a four-inch thick ironwood branch with a hole through it. Now I knew why I did not get that deer! Ironwood is very hard and I was so close to it when I shot, that my scope looked right over the branch. The barrel of my rifle was dead center on that branch. I remembered that the buck had jumped up, running off with his tail down. He must have been hit with tiny pieces of wood and the spent bullet, but not enough to hurt him much.

The moral of this true story is do not count your chickens before they are hatched. Most all the game that I have hunted was dropped with one well-placed shot, that's why I did not even think of shooting at that deer again as it ran away.

A person who enjoys hunting with other men develops a kinship that lasts a lifetime and a feeling with nature that does not go away. It draws you closer to God, the Great Creator of all things. I have some very special hunting companions that will be a part of my inner circle of friends until I die. Ray Buckwalter and Walter Schmidt have a great love for the outdoors and they really concentrate on the hunt. When in camp, they gladly did their share. That is what a true sportsman is all about, and there was no profanity heard either.

In 1967, my friend Ray invited me to go to Colorado to hunt. He had been traveling out there for many years and invited me to go along. It was the beginning of many trips I would take to the same area to hunt. I have many fond memories of beautiful Colorado and the Rocky Mountains. On one of those trips, a friend and I climbed this high mountain. It took us at least two hours just to reach the top. We separated to different areas and I sat down for a while. Later two does walked over the top of the hill, followed by a big buck. I dropped the buck with one shot, dressed it out, and waited for my friend to come and help me. Mule deer bucks can easily weigh 275 to 300 pounds live weight.

As we began to drag this huge buck down the steep slopes, it got away from us and tumbled into a ditch that broke off the horns. Well, I thought, I can always glue the horns back on! I stuck the horns in my belt and we kept going. My friend said, "George, I will carry your gun for you, but I am too tired to help you drag it any more."

I kept going when suddenly the deer slid very fast and got away from me again. It dropped into a deep ditch. I was played out. I thought to myself, that deer can just stay in that hole because I cannot get down there and get back out. At least I had the horns, or so I thought. When I reached back to get the horns, I discovered that my belt was loose. The bottoms of my pants were torn and I had no horns. What a bad day that was! I did get my second deer a few days later. You were allowed to take two deer at that time.

On another hunting trip to Colorado, I had an unusual experience. There had been a very heavy snow earlier, and some snow slides or avalanches had cut some wide swaths through the aspen trees. It was almost impossible to get through the deep snow. We decided we must stay low and hunt under the pine and aspen trees. As I was stalking along, I thought I saw a big doe lying down under a large spruce tree. I looked through the scope, placed my finger on the trigger, and fired. However, the deer did not move. I walked down hill to the deer about a hundred yards away and I soon had a big surprise. I had hit the deer through the neck. The bullet came out and hit another deer in the head that was lying right beside the first one! I had two deer with one shot! Fortunately, you were allowed two deer during those seasons, and my hunt was over. I drug those two deer out and was happy because the next day it began to rain.

I remember another unusual hunt that took place in the woods above my house. It was the second week of buck season and I still did not have my deer. We had a deep snow earlier and then it rained on top of that and froze hard, so there was a crust to walk on which was quite slippery. Sometimes you would break through, which was not too good for stalking.

I decided to stay about a quarter of a mile from the house. Soon the sun came out, but it was cold. About ten thirty, I saw some deer coming across the woods below me. Soon they turned and came straight towards me and the first deer was a nice buck. I could hardly believe it when he saw me and turned sideways and stood there watching me.

I shot the buck right behind the front shoulder. He ran about a hundred feet and fell over. The does took off running up the hill. When I walked over to my 6-point buck, I heard this sound way above me. I looked, and I saw this deer sliding down the hill toward me. I said to myself, "I have never seen the like. This doe ran up the hill so fast, had a heart attack, and died!"

"Now what do I do?" I said to myself. "Nobody will believe me when I tell them it died of fright. I guess I will just clean it too." I could not immediately see any bullet holes. I just dragged the buck down to the garage, went back, got the doe, and skinned them both. As I looked real close at the doe, it appeared that a very tiny flat piece of lead hit the doe in front of its shoulder and cut into its lung, but you could hardly see a mark. I just processed it with the buck because I could not prove how it died.

One of my hunting trips took me to the Yukon Territories in 1979. It was my most expensive trip. My wife and I drove the van over 4000 miles one-way to a place called Dawson City. She stayed in a motel in that town while I went with the outfitter. We flew north near the Arctic Circle and hunted for ten days. I had an Indian guide named Pete. He was very impressed with my shooting. I shot a big moose with one shot from my 30.06. Pete said he never saw a moose shot with one shot. I said to Pete that I shot everything with just one shot, and I proved that to him later when I shot a big caribou with one shot. We used a Super Cub airplane to fly to the general hunting area. Those pilots are crazy! They take chances that make your hair stand on end!

One day we flew north from camp and landed on the sandy beach as it curved around the trees. Anyone knows that you land and take off in a strait line, but in the Yukon you land around curves and up hill on a mountain. After I shot my caribou, we tied the horns to the struts that help to hold the wings on, put the meat inside, crawled in and down the mountain we went.

I thought that this was the end of a great hunt and I was going to die in that airplane. We were going down hill at a steep angle and I thought to myself—there is no way to get the tail of this plane off the ground. The trees were getting closer, but the engine roared and we just cleared the trees! I guess when you are the pilot, you learn what your plane can do. The outfitter would put a propane heater under the cowling of the plane, cover it with canvas, and leave it there all night so the engine would start the next morning.

The temperature was very cold the last few days of that hunt. I remember one morning when the temperature was well below zero. I carried water in two buckets from the creek nearby to the cook's cabin. The water froze on the top in the bucket, and when you looked close, there were tiny black bugs swimming around in that frigid water! How could they possibly live?

Later as my wife and I were driving home through British Colombia I said to her, "Let's stop and fry some of those caribou back straps and enjoy them for breakfast."

Now the hunting outfitter told me that the caribou were in the rutting season and the meat would have a bad taste when we ate it. I could not see anything wrong with the meat, so we fried some. That is when I learned what the outfitter meant. The meat tasted just like pee smells and it left a bad taste in my mouth that made me burp repeatedly. We realized that we must throw all of that meat away and we did. I hope that the wolves found it and had a feast.

In 1981, I decided to go on another hunt to Quebec for caribou. I wanted to take my son-in-law along, too. I arranged with an outfitter in the area and he got our licenses. I persuaded two more fellows into going along. There was an Amish friend of mine who wanted to go too, but his church leaders felt at that time that big game hunting trips were a waste of time and money, so they put pressure on him to forget about it. When the morning came to pick him up to head north to Canada, he said, "I guess that I can't go along with you fellows hunting. The church leaders said that I should stay home with my family!" I knew that he hurt inside real bad to go along, but we left without him. The four of us drove north a two-day journey to a small town along the St. Lawrence River called "Sep-tiles". There we got on a small jet plane to fly straight north to a small town named Shefferville to meet the outfitter and hunt for one week. Now we were almost 2000 miles from home. Did I ever get a shock when I got on that jet plane and found my Amish friend that we had left at home sitting on one of the seats! To make a long story short he said that he decided to forget what his church elders said. He went to Harrisburg Airport and caught the first plane from there to Shefferville, Quebec.

I have had many hunting adventures in my lifetime. I have taken twenty plus deer in Pennsylvania, and that many in Colorado, a six by six 44-inch bull elk, two large caribou, two moose, two beautiful antelope, plus deer from Wyoming and Manitoba. I made three trips to Manitoba, one that is worth sharing. The first year there, I shot a nice 8 point buck. When I filled out the tag, I marked the wrong day. This turned out to be a real trial. When we came out of the woods to our staging area, a game warden was there. I did not think anything about it as he checked our licenses. When he saw my tag that was punched out a day early, he got the idea that I must have shot a deer the day before. Now here I was out hunting again and shooting another deer. I tried to explain to him my honest mistake, as did the outfitter, too. He then took my rifle, my deer, and me to the game warden's office. There I sat for three hours while he and his friends figured out what to do with me. I was hunting with "Big Antler Outfitters." Around 11:30 pm that night, my outfitter named Ron came and tried to reason with him. He told the warden that it was an honest mistake and it was not very nice to treat his clients the way he was treating me. After much secret talks the warden left me go. I got my rifle, and my deer back. It was a learning experience.

I do not do as much hunting as I used to do because I have seen the needs of poor children in the countries that I have visited over the years. I feel a little guilty if I spend too much money on myself. Jesus said, "Do unto others as you would have them do unto you." That carries a lot of weight.

My hunting friends on a trip to northern Manitoba for whitetailed deer.

Trophy antelope taken in Wyoming, 2000.

CHAPTER 20

Fish Tales

One time when we lived in Ohio, one of the fellows that I worked with asked me if I like to fish. I shared with him about my fishing in the little creek for minnows back home on the farm.

He said, "How about going with me to Lake Erie to catch big perch?"

A few days later, we took his boat to Lake Erie to fish for perch. It was a beautiful day, and we caught a lot of perch. The fish were so plentiful that we used a spreader bar with a short line and hook. Before long, we were catching two at a time!

I had no idea that this kind of fishing existed and could be so much fun. The fish were 14 to 16 inches long and good to eat. Thus began the first of many great fishing trips during the next 45 years.

My neighbor in Ohio, Carl Mutter, asked me to go with him to Quebec to fish for walleye and northern pike. We drove from Massillon, Ohio to North Bay, Ontario. From there, we hired an outfitter to fly us east into Quebec where the guide had cabins furnished with bunk beds, kitchen utensils, and two boats. All we needed were our poles and food.

It was a real experience to wake up in the morning and hear the ducks and loons calling. We saw moose along the lake. However, we did not see any planes overhead and had no telephone or television. There were no other human beings around, not even a woman to cook for us. I asked the pilot later about that and he said, "You should have told me and I would have brought a young woman for your cooking and enjoyment."

Carl and I said, "We needed to just be alone, us and God."

We caught lots of walleye and some nice pike. The walleye tasted so much better, so I fried lots of fish for our meals during our week there.

One morning as we stood on the dock, I said to Carl, "I declare I hear a waterfall some where."

He said, "You are hearing things. It is flat around here."

I said, "I am going toward that sound. We have all day to find it."

We took off in our boat, traveling for a while, and then stopping the motor to listen. Later we found a small lake maybe forty feet higher than the lake where we were fishing. The sound I heard was a waterfall!

We found an old path up to the small lake and an old iron track that was used long ago to portage small boats up to that lake. This was very interesting to us. I told Carl, "I'll bet no one fishes up here. Let's see if there are any fish in this water."

We got our poles and went back up the trail. I cast out near a patch of lily pads. When my lure hit the water, I noticed the lily pads moving. I said, "Carl, there is something in here."

The next cast a big pike grabbed my lure and took off fighting. I got it turned around and began to reel it in. At the same time, I walked backwards up the bank dragging the fish up on the bank! To make a long story short, I have that 32-inch pike mounted and hanging on my office wall.

George and northern pike caught in Quebec.

After we moved back to Pennsylvania from Ohio, I made several more trips to Quebec and Ontario fishing with my friends. I remember one trip with Eugene Glick, John Smith, and his son. We drove north from Belleville to a town in northern Quebec called Chibugamu. We stayed in a cabin and then went out to the nearby lake early in the morning.

One day as we were fishing, it became very windy. The fish quit biting, and we began to drift around a point into shallow water. We had two boats: Eugene and I were in one boat, and John and his son were in another boat. We had radios so we could talk to each other if we got separated. I told Eugene, "I do not like this strong wind. Let's drift behind that sand bar over those reeds close to the bank." I lifted the motor up so it would not hit the bottom.

I told Eugene, "We probably will not catch fish here. The water is only 30 inches deep." Nevertheless, since we were there, I threw my line over in the shallows just for fun. A walleye grabbed the jig. Eugene looked at me with surprise as I pulled a 14-inch fish into the boat! He cast out his line and right away hooked a walleye too.

He radioed John, "Get over here out of the wind. The fish are in this shallow water!"

We talked about that excitement for many years and the joy of eating all those fresh fried fillets between two slices of bread with butter back at the cabin.

On another trip, I traveled to Canada with Aaron Peachey, Willard Yoder, Roland Yoder, and two other fellows whose names I cannot recall. We drove from Belleville to a town in Quebec called Senneterre.

There we parked the car at the train station, boarded a train, and went east for eighty miles or more. The train stopped at a small crossing and we got off. We boarded an old bus to go the rest of the way. We arrived at a fishing camp called Kapatachawan Club, where we met two French brothers. They operated a first rate camp with the finest fishing setup that I had seen in a long time. I saw five clean log cabins with four beds each, and a separate large building where we would go for our meals. We had Indian guides, who operated boats with 25 horsepower motors.

At nine o'clock in the morning, we would get into the boats. The guides would take us to the hot spots, tell us what type of lures to use, and get them in the water! We soon found out that the fish were hungry. Walleyes were the name of the game there. Sometimes we would catch a pike, but the guides called them snakefish and would not keep them to eat.

At noontime, we would stop miles from the main camp. The guides would clean some of the walleyes we caught and fry them over an open fire. They would cook some corn or baked beans and serve bread and butter. We would take two slices of bread and two fillets of fish, add some catsup, and eat until we could not eat anymore! It was a time to sit around the fire and share stories with the Indian guides, plus swat some hungry mosquitoes. Then we would go out and catch some more fish. Around five o'clock, we would arrive back at camp, where the guides would clean the fish, and put them on ice.

A small building housed a shower room with a large tank on top of the roof. Water was pumped out of the lake during the day and heated. By the time we came back from fishing, we could enjoy a hot shower. At six o'clock, we sat down to eat a full course meal while we visited.

Flounder caught along the coast of Florida.

My friend Willard caught a 32-inch walleye that he had mounted. Aaron was with me one afternoon when he hooked a big 43-inch pike in very shallow water. Another evening I hooked something very big but it did not act like any other fish I had hooked before. It just took off in a big circle and tore the line. The fellows said that they believed it was a lake trout, but I wished I could have seen what it was.

I went on several more trips to that same lodge. I would highly recommend it for fisherman that want to enjoy the easy life. It was interesting to see how the men would cut large blocks of ice out of the lake in the winter and take them to the icehouse via a conveyer belt. There the ice was covered with sawdust and kept all summer long.

I went on several trips to the Chesapeake Bay area, to Barnegat Light on the coast of New Jersey, and to the Indian River Inlet in Delaware. The only problem with ocean fishing is seasickness. I suffered from it so badly several times that I wished I could die. If you have ever experienced it, you know what I mean. I used to get carsick when I was a kid, but it never bothers me when I am driving. Maybe I have outgrown it.

In 1986, I purchased a sixteen-foot aluminum boat and mounted a 20-horse power motor. Now I had my own boat. My wife and I made many trips to Sarasota, Lake Okeechobee, and a few other spots in Florida. We also made many trips to a lake in New York called Chautauqua Lake, which has so many fish it is known as the most productive fishery in New York. Every year we travel to this lake during the middle of July and stay in a small fishing motel owned by Pat and Bob Brown in Bemis Point. There are pike, walleyes, large and small mouth bass, white perch, yellow perch, sunfish, bluegills, and more.

This lake has an average depth of ten to twelve feet with lots of weed beds around the edges. Many anglers travel there to try for big muskies, and there are lots of them in the lake. Katie and I caught more

Katie with walleye caught at
Chautauqua Lake, NY.

fish in this lake than all the other places combined!
I average around 25 quarts of frozen fillets every
year.

One time, as my wife and I were fishing at
Chautauqua Lake, I cast my line with a big worm on
a hook near a place where a mother duck with her
young were floating. Just as the bait hit the water,
one of the small ducks dove under the water and
grabbed the worm. I quickly pulled the line back,
but the duck got the hook caught in its bill. I reeled

in the line as the duck splashed around. The other ducks came to investigate and the mother duck swam over and quacked, trying to free her baby. It was an exciting time until I reeled the duck close enough to the boat to free it. When I released the duck, the other ducks chased it all the way to the shore, plus the mother duck chased after it and gave it a good scolding. This may sound like a tall tale, but my wife and I got a good laugh out of it.

One year our daughter Nancy, her husband Jim, our two granddaughters, and Jim's parents, Clair and Leona Williams, traveled to the lake to visit with us and do some fishing. Jim, Lenette, Clair, and I went to a good spot where I thought we might catch a fish. Lenette was eight years old at the time, and using a little Mickey Mouse rod with a small jig on her line. Suddenly she said, "Daddy, my line is pulling hard. Would you help me?" He helped her hold on to the pole, and finally the two of them reeled a big bass near the boat, where I netted it for her. What an exciting time for her two grandpas to see her catch a trophy fish! She had her picture taken with her big bass, and it appeared in a New York fishing magazine. Jim had the fish mounted, and it now hangs on a wall of their home.

I would like to share a strange tale about a fish in Colorado. My friend Ray Buckwalter and I were hiking along a trail about two miles back into a canyon while on a hunting trip. There was a small stream flowing down the gully about 60 yards from the trail. As the sun came up behind us, we looked down over the side to the stream. We noticed what appeared to be a big fish in a small pool. Ray and I laid our hunting rifles down and took out our binoculars to look at this big fish! We wondered how in the world it ever got there and how it survived in the winter. It appeared to be at least fourteen inches long or more. I said to Ray that I wanted to check it out when we came back down in the evening.

That night, just as the sun was going down, we came down the trail and I crawled down over the bank trying to be careful that the fish would not see me. Well, I sure came to a shocking conclusion when I saw the fish. It was a bright red mountain trout maybe four-inches long at the most. We decided that the sun shining on the pool in the morning had magnified it to giant proportions. That was a time I was fooled by a fish.

As I think about different experiences in my Florida fishing days and all the hundreds of live shrimp that I put on hooks to catch sheep head, sugar trout, sea trout, snook, redfish, or whiting, it would take many pages to tell about it. One time as I fished off of the Sarasota Bay Bridge, I caught a nice big trout! When I pulled it out of the water, a pelican grabbed and swallowed my fish. Well I just kept on pulling, and I pulled that trout right out of the pelican's throat. I cheated that bird out of a meal! Katie and I caught hundreds of crappies in Lake Okeechobee. I caught a big snook under the Stickney Point Bridge.

Many years ago, I joined the Coffee Run Fishing Club located about six miles from my house. I enjoyed time spent together with other men building fish rearing ponds and dams. We would buy hundreds of small trout and feed them for two years, then stock them in the stream for a while before fishing season would begin. We had 100 members in the club. Although many fellows would not show up for activities, they would help stock the stream.

CHAPTER 21

Having a Blast

I remember in my early teen years, my foster mother telephoning a man named Alphie Glick. She asked him to come to the farm and dynamite some big rocks out of the ground. She wanted to cultivate this one field along the foot of the mountain, but it had a few very large sandstones. I asked Mother if I could go along with Alphie and watch. I was now introduced to a whole new world of excitement. Mr. Glick was not a young man and sometimes he would call Mother and ask if I could go along to help carry his tools and things.

When I worked for J.M. Young & Sons, one of the owners, David Young, did all their blasting work. I bought all of his equipment when he retired. During that time, farmers could buy some explosives for their own use on the farms. Soon, however, a new law went into effect that all people who wanted to continue their blasting work had to go to the state capital to take a written and oral test. I took the test, passed it, and got my license. The license only cost $3.50 a year! I maintained that license from 1962 until 1998, even when I lived in Ohio.

In the early days, some of the local feed mills would stock fifty-pound cases of dynamite. I would go to Mapleton Depot, Pennsylvania, and buy what I needed. However, with these new laws, they did not want to be liable for any stolen explosives. I then purchased my stuff right from the manufacturer. I did a lot of blasting work during those years and I had some wild times or should I say interesting things that I did with explosives! Some farmers would call me to blast old sewer pits so they would drain better. I was called a lot of times to blast stumps and the farmer would say, put lots of powder under it so it would fly all around and then we would laugh! I made a drill about five feet long to bore under big boulders and that was just the right size to blast them out.

I blasted ground hog holes, and several times in the late forties, I would make miniature bombs with a little glass bottle. I would punch a small hole in the lid, cut a five inch piece of fuse, crimp a cap on it, light that, and throw it in the deep holes in the creek. This would make the fish turn belly up! I wanted to see what would happen to pigeons if you took a blasting cap, a short piece of fuse, fasten that to a pigeon, and let it fly. About the time that the bird was up in the sky, there would be a bang and feathers would fall to the ground. It seemed that boys would catch pigeons and call me just to see this event. As I look back at those times, I get a sad feeling in my heart for those pigeons. We would never do this kind of thing now.

We now have rockets that we shoot at enemy planes in war times. One time I took a load of logs to a sawmill owned by Emanuel Byler. He was blasting a stump out in the pasture field, so I went over to watch. When he lit the fuse, his dog jumped on top of the stump and began to bark at the smoke! Well, when we ran away from the stump, the dog just stayed there and no amount of coaxing could get the dog off of the stump.

Suddenly the stump flew in the air and that dog bounced off and ran to the barn terrified! It was amazing to us that the dog could still run! We could not help but laugh like crazy. Later Emanuel said he could not get the dog to go with him to blast stumps anymore.

By the late 1980s, rules were getting so strict that many license holders could not keep up with the new laws and crazy regulations. For instance, one rule stated that you had to blow your car horn three times before you set off a blast. You also had to report on what the weather was like and file a traffic plan. You could not park your car within 300 feet of a restaurant or 400 feet of a bridge without having someone with you to watch your truck when it contained explosives. You had to fill out a twenty-question paper questionnaire even if you went just a couple of miles from home to blast a stump along a fencerow. I was even fined $2,000 for not obeying a rule that I did not even know existed! I eventually got so disgusted, that I said, "Forget it." I did not need all the hassle and the paperwork. I am sure this is what the government wanted anyway!

While I did a lot of blasting work in those years, I also got into the enjoyment of setting off fireworks at county fairs and festivals. I began to do this in 1962 and I had more fun lighting up the night sky with beautiful lights and lots of noise. The people of Mifflin County enjoyed my displays for many years, but I have quit doing this now.

I decided that there are other things to get a blast out of in life besides dynamiting and fireworks. I still have all of my fingers and toes and that is a lot more than many men can say. Many a man was killed doing this type of work.

I must share an interesting story that took place during my blasting career. In 1995, a man from Lemont, Pennsylvania, contacted me, asking if I could help him open a mausoleum to remove a casket, which was built in 1928. The mausoleum was located near Lewistown and was constructed out of concrete and stones with four-feet thick walls on all sides. The top was encased with blocks of white marble imported from Italy with eighteen-feet long slabs for the roof. The tomb was built for a very wealthy man from the Lewistown area who was going to build another one for his wife. In the meantime, he and his wife had a fall out and she did not want to be buried beside him, so she was buried in the cemetery at Lewistown.

In the middle nineties, his heirs wanted to move his

casket to another location in the Juniata Memorial Park beside his wife. The heirs hired a man by the name of Mays from Lemont who sold monuments. They made an agreement with him to remove the casket from this mausoleum in exchange for the white marble casing that covered the entire tomb. Mr. Mays had spent almost three thousand dollars and had not been able to get through the thick walls. He asked me if I could blast the concrete walls apart. I looked at the job and decided to try. Then he said he did not have much time or money left, because he had a deadline to meet.

I asked him what he was going to do with those large white marble slabs that encased the tomb. He said that he was hoping to sell them for tombstones. I asked what he planned to ask for one stone. He quoted me a price of $700 each. I said that I would exchange my services for a tombstone for my wife and me. He said he would gladly make a tombstone if I could get that casket out without any damage. So, it was a done deal!

I blasted the rocks loose and I had my friend Sam Hostetler, who owns Sam's Backhoe Service, shred the remaining stone and concrete with his track-hoe. We lifted the casket out of that large tomb and it did not take very long. My total cost was $220. The man was so excited that it was done so quickly. He made our tombstone and I installed it in the cemetery at Allensville Mennonite Cemetery where it marks our final resting place. Have you ever heard of using a second hand stone, especially one from Italy? The next time you pass by the cemetery, you may see the white marble tombstone. Remember this story from my book!

CHAPTER 22

My Traveling Days

As a young boy, when I would go out early in the morning to chase the cows in to be milked, I would look up at the bright moon as it went down behind the mountain into Stone Valley. I would think to myself, "Some day I am going up to the top of that mountain and see where the moon is going. I want to find out how far it is and go walk on it!"

Later in school as we studied the stars and the moon, one of the books said that the moon was somewhere around 110,000 miles away from us. I decided it would take a lot longer to get there than I thought. As I got older, I wanted to go places. I wanted to go to every country in the world.

As a child, I remember saying something to someone that must not have sounded sensible because the person looked at me with a stare and said, "Why don't you go take a ride on a galloping goose!" I studied that for a bit and I decided that was not the way I wanted to travel.

In the early 1960's, America was experimenting with big rockets that could shoot men up high in the sky. I was very excited about that and I would carry my little radio along to work so I could listen to the space travel experiences. One day I well remember, when America sent the first man named John Glenn, up into the blue sky. He was supposed to fall back to earth. When he had reached the highest point that he wanted to be, he started to fall back down. The man on the radio lost contact with the man in the space capsule. Every one began to think that it caught fire and burned up! I stopped working to listen and was I ever glad when radio contact was made again. I thought I might be able to go to the moon after all some day! Now many years later, America has sent men to the moon and they have come back with very exciting stories. They even brought rocks and ground back to study. I guess I will not go to the moon after all. I am too old for that now.

In January of 1973, I was coming home from work and something happened to me that changed my life! The roads were very icy and I came upon an accident. A motorist lost control of her car, spinning, ending up with the front end on top of the guardrails, blocking part of the road. I stopped to check if anyone was injured. The passengers were okay, so I put flares out along the road to warn traffic. As I bent down to set the flare, another car came around the curve and spun out on the ice hitting me! The force threw me against the guardrails, breaking my upper arm. I needed two bone grafts to get it back to health so I was not able to work for my employer, like I wanted to.

During that healing period, some of my Amish friends asked me if I could drive my work van. I said that I could, and they said that they need someone to take them places to do some business. I put my two extra seats back into my van that I had removed for work projects.

I started to drive them around the country while my arm was in a cast. I enjoyed that so much that I soon saw that this was something that I enjoyed and it was curing the desire to travel! I eventually told my employer that I was giving him a two-week work notice and I would go see the world and get paid for it at the same time. On June 1, 1974, I began to take my friends and others on short trips around the state and soon into other states. I made trips into California and Canada.

One trip I must tell about was a trip I took in 1975. At that time, the country was experiencing a gas shortage. You had to go to the gas station early and the stations would close around 9 or 10 a.m. I decided to go out to my former employer in Ohio and buy a 275 gallon fuel oil tank and lay it in the back of the van in the horizontal position, brace it firm and then fill it full of gas. It seemed so funny to have a big tank truck back up to my van and fill this big tank. We put two hundred sixty gallons in that tank and took off for a long trip through the south west and down to Florida.

We visited my former employer from Ohio, who had a beautiful home in West Palm Beach, Florida. Mr. Campbell said to me, "How can you get gas to travel all over the country since it is so hard to get?"

I told him how I had stopped at his company office in Ohio and purchased a 275-gallon tank and put inside the van filled with high-test gas! He said, "You rascal! Here I am in Florida without any gas and you are vacationing all over the country with gas in one of my tanks!" We had a laugh about that. I said that we could siphon some out for him. I often think what a horrible fire there would have been if we had been in an accident.

Another trip that was especially exciting was a three-week run in 1978 taking some Amish friends south into Central America. I took a load of folks from Kentucky, south into Texas, and into Mexico. We followed route A1.A through Guatemala and San Salvador into Honduras. We stayed there a week and then drove back again to our homes. While I was there, I built a brick chimney for David Peachey. I must say that going through all those border crossings got to be a real headache, because we had to unload the van to the bare floor. Two of my passengers were Esther Peachey and Jo-Ann Miller. They were 18 or 19 years old. When the border guards saw these beautiful girls, they forgot about their responsibilities and wanted to talk to them. It sure made for some amusement.

The Amish people living in Honduras opened an orphanage for Spanish children. One of the reasons for this trip was to take supplies, including quilts, electric tools, twenty-five pound blocks of chocolate, and a variety of other things for poor people. I had purchased a book from Sanborn Travel Agency in Dallas, Texas, that told me all about the road layouts and commonly used Spanish words in Central America. We had to stay calm while the border guards looked through all this stuff. We did this every time as we came to the border of each country. Then we would go over to the other side of the border and do it all over again, because the next country wanted to see what we were bringing in!

That was a real trip. Not knowing the language and the area, plus going through all the border crossings with that red tape was a challenge. It was a great learning experience and I would do it again. After I crossed the borders of other countries back into the United States, I got down on my knees and kissed the ground because I was safe in the good old USA! Then my friends said to me, "Please go and find the nearest Dairy Queen. We are starving for milk shakes!"

I did a lot of traveling like this with people to every state in the U.S. except Alaska.

In 1976, some of our local Lions Club members decided to travel to Hawaii for the international convention. We joined a larger group of over 200 people who had chartered a plane from Pittsburgh. The trip was great fun. We took our daughter Nancy and her friend Rhoda Hostetler along for company. We stayed in Waikiki for a week and enjoyed the warm water plus lots of Polynesian food. I even danced with some hula girls. They are very beautiful with long black hair, big brown eyes, and a natural tan.

In 1981 between trips, I was doing some plumbing

and electric work. I became very busy, so I was not traveling as much. Then in 1986, I said to myself, I have been all over North America and I have not had any major problems. I have so much work right around home that I believe that God wants me to take a break from traveling. I shall sell my van and stay at home for a while.

In 1983, a member of our Allensville Mennonite church asked me if I would like to go to Japan. Lee and Adella Kanagy spent over 20 years in Japan doing mission work and were now living back in our area. My wife and I thought about this and we decided to go with them and some other friends.

In May, we traveled to Korea and Japan on a three-week trip. Now this was something very special, because we went to the world's largest church in Seoul, South Korea, visited the Emperor's palace, and toured other historic places in that country for several days. After that, we flew to Japan and visited many places all over that country. We rode the fast trains that go over 200 miles an hour. We went to Buddhist temples and other shrines. We visited Hiroshima, the city that had been blown up by an atom bomb, which left quite an impression on me. As I look back over the terrible calamity that can come to humankind, what a pity that people do not learn to love the God who made them. The evil spirit of Satan will govern us, if we do not follow Christ and His love!

We made some wonderful friends as we traveled over northern Japan. We stayed in some people's homes and learned to sit on the floor to eat our meals, which included some foods that we do not eat at home! We had to learn to eat with chopsticks. Katie and I experienced our first earthquake while we were in Japan. One morning as we were still resting in our beds, the bedroom door began to shake. Katie said there was someone at the door. I said, "No, that was an earthquake!" The earth was rumbling and we were getting scared. Just then, the homeowner came to our door and said everything was okay. It definitely was a new experience.

Our guide, Lee, had started several Mennonite churches in Japan and we visited some of those churches. We met many wonderful people, but I hate to say that only around 2-3 percent of Japan's population follows after Jesus Christ! I say to myself, when will they ever learn?

In 1991, we continued our travel adventures. We went on a seven-day sea cruise from Miami, Florida, to the Cayman Islands, Cozamel, Jamaica, and other places. We traveled with my brother, Bob, and his wife, Donna. It was a wonderful time together and brings back many good memories.

In 1993, we took another sea cruise to Bermuda for six days with Bob and Donna. I was impressed how the beaches were of a pink color and the water was so warm. The sunbathers wore very little and some people wore nothing. I thought to myself, this is the way we would have all walked around if Adam and Eve had not sinned!

God had another plan for my life. In November of 1992, one of my friends in our church asked me if I would like to go with him to Russia. I said, "Russia! You can't go to Russia; that's a communist country."

However, he said, "Communism has collapsed there and people can now go visit." He told me about a humanitarian aid organization, Josh McDowell Ministry, based in Dallas, Texas. "They are looking for volunteers to go to Russia to distribute medical supplies, school supplies, gospel literature and lots of Bibles!"

I said, "How much does it cost to go?"

He said, "$2,200 for two weeks." I talked to my wife about going.

She said, "That would be very interesting to do, but you go. I don't want to go that far away." At that time Katie had problems with high blood pressure and the doctor did not recommend her to fly so far from home.

I decided to go with my friend to Russia. At least I would be in a country that I never thought I could

Josh McDowell, President of Josh McDowell Ministries, with Katie and I.

go to. I looked at the map of Russia and saw that it really is on the other side of the globe. I packed my suitcase with plenty of winter clothing because we were going in January.

Our group consisted of more than 300. We were told that we would go to public schools, orphanages, and hospitals to distribute a variety of school supplies, medical equipment, and food that was purchased in Holland and Germany and shipped to Moscow earlier. Russia was going through a major change in their political world as communism had collapsed in 1989 and their money was almost worthless. In 1989, a ruble was equivalent to one of our quarters. By the time we were there in 1993, it changed to 620 rubles to the dollar!

We passed out gospel literature, bibles, and a book written by Josh McDowell entitled *More Than A Carpenter* all printed in Russian. I felt a little apprehensive about giving this out on the street in a big city and in a faraway country, but this was partly why we came to Russia. The people had to burn all their bibles and religious things seventy years earlier due to the communist governments demands. We split into small groups of six people and began to pass out the books at street corners and bus stops. I soon got over my apprehension. When the people saw us giving out free stuff, they grabbed the books from us and wanted more to give to their friends. Our group was in shock as we passed out more than 1500 books in twenty minutes. Just like passing out food to starving people, we passed out spiritual food to starving souls! I can guarantee that we were in the right place, at the right time. Jesus said that the harvest was ready and we were the reapers.

This was just the beginning of an exciting two weeks. We shared pictures of our families and homes in America to many adults and children in the schools and other places as we went. You just cannot imagine how the people welcomed us. During distribution times at many schools, we were served different kinds of food, tea, and coffee. We talked about Jesus, God's Son, and how he died on the cross for our sins, making a way for us to have a relationship with God, our Father. We had Russian young people with us that understood English, who acted as interpreters. We also played a cassette tape to the children that explained to them about a gospel bead bracelet that we gave to each child to keep. They also received the story about the bracelet in a pamphlet so they could remember it. We asked the children to pray with us to receive Jesus into their hearts, and they did!

I will always remember a day we went to a big public school. We had just finished distributing all our things to over three hundred children, when we were asked to come into a room to talk with the teachers and the school superintendent. I wondered what was going to happen now. A stern woman, she began to tell us that our visit to her school was just unbelievable. Many years before when she became the superintendent, she thought no one would ever say anything about God in her school. Now here we were doing this very thing. She could not believe that we would come so far from America just to give things to all the children, and gifts to the teachers, and how we told them the gospel story. Well, she just broke down, cried, and hugged us and we hugged her and the teachers. I get misty eyed as I am writing this because the love of Jesus had just come to this school, and I played a part in it.

One day our schedule took us to a Russian nursing home. This was a real eye opener. We saw three buildings that looked more like old storage sheds. We went inside and found a lot of elderly people living there. One building had many old women, another section housed a lot of old men. I was asked by my leader to speak to the men. They gathered in one large room and I began to speak about the reason why we were there. I asked God to quickly tell me what to say, because these were old men that maybe one time had fought against us, and did not like us there.

I told them that some of the best chess players came from Russia and God forgives what happened in the past when you ask him, and that I was so glad that I had the opportunity to visit with them. I shared about my life, and how God has blessed us and we wanted to give them each some gifts of books, games, and candy bars. I was sad for them, yet I received a great blessing as they gave me hugs and smiles, and a few trinkets that they had made. Your life is never the same after an experience like that.

We shared the gospel wherever we went, and made many friends as we visited a few homes and experienced their culture. We had the chance to go to the world famous Bolshoy Theatre and watch the ballet, Swan Lake. There were thirty-six beautiful ballerinas dancing at one time. We went shopping at a big flea market in Moscow, and I purchased a lot of things to bring back home. Russia is a very big country, with eleven time zones. It takes two weeks to go from the west end to the east end by train! I came home from this wonderful trip with great memories, but I decided that I wanted to travel to other countries next time.

However, God had other plans for me. The next year in January 1994, I was asked by the same organization to travel with them to Russia again. Since that time, I have traveled to Russia twelve times, including two summer trips. I have also traveled eight times to Belarus, which was a part of the USSR years ago. In 1995, this organization asked me if I would join with them as an affiliate staff person and cover central Pennsylvania for their mission work. I have been a member of their mission board now for eight years.

I want to say that four of my mission trips to Belarus have been on my own. On one trip to Belarus, we visited a baby orphanage that was so poor some of the babies had no diapers. They were feeding the

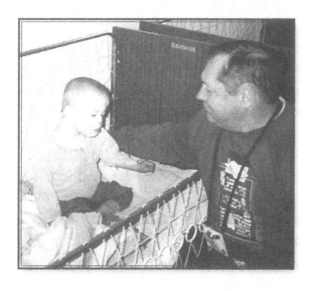

Visiting children in a Russian disabled children's hospital.

babies with a rubber hose stuck in a soda bottle because they did not have nursing bottles! That really bothered me. I decided that when I got home, I would get some baby supplies together and take them back to that orphanage.

In the summer of 2000, I packed five large suitcases full of baby things and drove to the Dulles International Airport near Washington DC. As I was checking my luggage in at the Lufthansa ticket counter, one of the women at the counter said, "What are you doing with five suitcases!"

I knew that you are usually allowed two suitcases, but if you are taking humanitarian aid to Europe, you may take three suitcases free one way. I knew that it would cost me quite a bit of money for those two extra suitcases.

I told the women that my suitcases were full of baby supplies for a poor orphanage in Belarus. They gave me my ticket to board the plane. As I reached for my boarding pass, one of the women quickly took it back and said to the other woman, "Isn't that a wonderful thing he is doing. Let's send him first class." Instead of sitting in the back of the plane, I sat up front with the rich and famous! It goes to show that you never know what God has in store for you! I still go to Belarus with baby supplies for orphanages and hospitals as often as I can. As of 2004, I have made twenty trips across the Atlantic Ocean to Western Europe. There will be a need for these items for years to come.

In the summer of 2002, I raised over $8,000 through my church and friends. I also borrowed $6,000 from my bank. Then I went to Belarus for a month to build a church in a small town called Gorodishe. I did not have enough time to build it all at that time, so I plan to go back for a month next year and try to finish it. The church project is very near and dear to my heart. I feel that God has called me to help these people have a place to worship.

I some times wonder if I would qualify as an ambassador to Russia. I went to the capital of Russia several times and to central Siberia and other remote towns. People there have very little money. A truck comes around once a week and exchanges flour, sugar, salt, and other necessities for cabbage, potatoes, carrots, and a few other things that the poor people can barter or exchange.

I know that everything in America is not perfect by a long shot, but we have more here than any other country that I know of. It was so bad in the early nineties in Russia that single women asked me several times if I would please just marry them while I was in their country. Then they could come back to the United States with me and I could divorce them. At least they would be free, because they have no future in their country! I feel so bad for the young people that finish college. There is no work for them and many girls sell their bodies just to buy food and survive.

God has solved my traveling urges, but I really want to see Alaska yet. I would like to suggest to readers to go see the world when you are young if you can afford it, because you may be too stiff and sore when you are old!

Katie and I visited many popular big name churches, including The Glass Cathedral in California, the

Tower of Power and Oral Roberts University in Tulsa, Okalahoma, The Mormon Tabernacle in Salt Lake City, Utah, and several more.

Cathedral of Jesus Christ Our Savior,
largest cathedral in Moscow, Russia.

CHAPTER 23

The Tale End

I am finding out that the idea of retiring from work is not an easy task, at least for me. I have come to a firm conclusion that when a man as diversified in his jobs as I have been, reaches retirement, it is different than for someone who has worked in a factory all his life. Suddenly retirement comes and he says goodbye to all his fellow workers and walks out the door and that is it!

In my case, there is a continuing saga of the phrase, "Could you do this for me? We can't find anyone that has time to come now!" So here I go again and I am working.

People say, "I thought you were retired!"

Then I say, "Yes, I thought I was retired, too, but I do not know what from!" I was told that I will be retired when the undertaker carries me out the front door, so until then I will do things for folks as I can.

I am in good health although I get a little pain in my left hip. The doctor says that a little arthritis has settled in and some pain pills may take care of that.

My wife's memory is beginning to fail her. For quite awhile, I noticed something going wrong. Eight years ago, I told her she must pay better attention to people's phone calls and write all the numbers down when people called. I could not return phone calls with only five or six digit numbers! I was not aware that something was going wrong with her brain cells.

One day as I was driving down the road, I was listening to the radio and the speaker was talking about people who have a condition called Dementia. He said that you want to try to get those people back in the same frame of mind that they used to be but that is not possible. I really needed to hear that speaker because it put me in a much different frame of mind.

Katie has reached the point that she cannot be left alone in the house or she may start to cry. I do all the cooking, sweeping the house, and help her to get dressed. She wakes me up in the early morning hours and is full of questions. She may start to whimper and say that she does not know where she is. I say, "Why, honey, you are right beside me in bed."

"Okay," she says. But that answer may be okay for a minute or so, then another question comes along. I just do not get much rest after four o'clock in the morning. People say that Dementia is the worst disease that a person can get, because there is no cure.

There is a statement made on your wedding day by the preacher when he says, "For better or worse, till death do you part." We must never forget that. I cared for my wife for many years in our cottage at Valley View Retirement Community. In March of 2004, my daughter and I placed Katie in the nursing home facility. I am still able to take her out occasionally for outings, but I realize the day is coming soon when she may not even know who I am.

My wife, Katie, and I in 2004.

When I leave this world I want to leave a legacy that would say, "owe no man anything but to love one another." Life is short. You are soon forgotten. A tombstone in the Allensville Mennonite Church Cemetery will show the world where George and Katie Mohler will be buried.

I hope that anyone who reads this book will be blessed by it and it will give you the desire to do the same for your family and your heritage.